نَسْتَعِينُ اهْدِنَا

الصِّرَاطَ الْمُسْتَقِيمَ

صِرَاطَ الَّذِينَ أَنْعَمْتَ

عَلَيْهِمْ غَيْرِ الْمَغْضُوبِ

عَلَيْهِمْ وَلَا الضَّالِّينَ

بِسْمِ اللَّهِ الرَّحْمَنِ الرَّحِيمِ
الْحَمْدُ لِلَّهِ رَبِّ الْعَالَمِينَ
الرَّحْمَنِ الرَّحِيمِ مَالِكِ
يَوْمِ الدِّينِ إِيَّاكَ
نَعْبُدُ وَإِيَّاكَ

Surah Al Fatihah
The Opening

"In the name of God, Most Gracious,
Most Merciful
Praise be to God, the Cherisher and
Sustainer of the Worlds;
Most Gracious, Most Merciful;
Master of the Day of Judgment.
Thee do we worship, and Thine aid we seek.
Show us the straight way,
The way of those on whomm
Thou hast bestowed Thy Grace,
those whose (portion) is not wrath,
and who go not astray"

The Holy Qur'an
Text and Translation by 'Abdullah Yusuf 'Ali

Previous double-page spread
Surah Al Fatihah
Ottoman bound Quran, Cat. no. 9, p. 43

In Memory of
Syed Nor Albukhary

Mightier
than the
Sword

Arabic script : beauty and meaning

This catalogue is published in conjunction with the exhibition "**Mightier than the Sword – Arabic script : beauty and meaning**", held at the Islamic Arts Museum Malaysia from 22 April 2004 – 20 July 2004.

The exhibition is organised by the Islamic Arts Museum Malaysia in collaboration with the British Museum UK.

Publisher :
The Islamic Arts Museum Malaysia

Authors :
Dr. Venetia Porter and Dr Heba Nayel Barakat
With contributions by Cecile Bresc

Editorial team :
Mina Koochekzadeh, Asma Shurfa Shukry and Nicola Kuok, Curatorial Affairs Department;
Puan Saadah Shaikh Mahmood, Marketing & Communication Department.
Islamic Arts Museum Malaysia

Design Director & Supervisor :
Aniza Ashaari, Graphic Unit; Islamic Arts Museum Malaysia

Designer :
Alnurmarida Alias; Graphic Unit; Islamic Arts Museum Malaysia

Photolab Photographers, Islamic Arts Museum Malaysia's Collection:
Syed Naqib Albar Syed Hamid
Faizal Zahari, Rizal Zaidi Zainudin

Colour separation, printing and binding :
DI Print Solutions Sdn Bhd

©2004 IAMM Publications
ISBN 983-40845-4-4

Thank You

Co-presenter

Co-sponsors

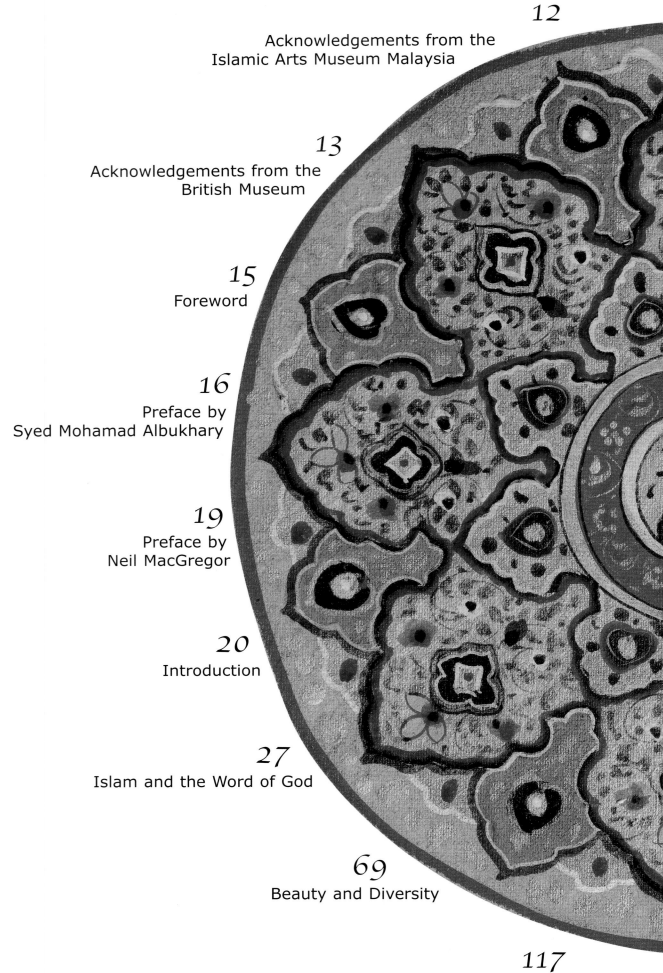

Acknowledgements from the Islamic Arts Museum Malaysia

The Islamic Arts Museum Malaysia would like to acknowledge the following persons without whom the exhibition and catalogue would not have been accomplished.

Our sincere appreciation goes to Neil MacGregor, the director of the British Museum for his enthusiasm and support of the exhibition, to Dr. Venetia Porter for all the dedication and effort she contributed in making this catalogue and exhibition a memorable event, to Maureen Theobald and Stephen Ruscoe, The British Museum.

Our special thanks are extended to our co-presenter, HSBC, an institution of 120 years of achievements within South East Asia and around the world. To Mr. Zarir J. Cama for foreseeing that HSBC continues to contribute in safeguarding and presenting cultural treasures to Malaysia.

Special thanks to our sponsors: RWE Power International and leading engineering services provider, The British High Commissioner Malaysia H. E. Bruce Cleghorn and Deputy High Commissioner Mr. Mark Canning, The British Council Director Mr. Gerry Liston, and to Tan Sri Dato Seri Azizan Zainul Abidin, Dato Md. Nor Yusof and Puan Jamilah Itam of Malaysian Airlines and MAS Kargo for their continuous support in promoting the arts and bringing to Malaysia educational and intellectual exhibitions.

We would also like to thank Puan Sri Sharifah Zarah Albukhary, Dr. Tom Craig-Cameron, the former director of the British Council, Malaysia, Mr. Alistair Duncan, Altajir World of Islam Trust, the inspiring artist Dr. Ahmed Moustafa, and Jabatan Kemajuan Islam Malaysia (JAKIM).

We would like to extend our appreciation to all IAMM staff for working as a team and Dr. Heba Nayel Barakat, our visiting Professor for all the research done for the catalogue of this 'Mightier than the Sword, Arabic script : Beauty and Meaning' exhibition.

Puan Sarifah Majimah Albukhary, Finance & Administration Dept.; Ms. Hamidah Non, Operation Dept.; Puan Saadah Shaikh Mahmood, Marketing & Communication Dept.; Puan Noridah Ghazali, Events Dept.; Mr. Choong Loy Fatt, Security Dept.; Mr. Zambre Md Yusoff, Maintenance Dept.; Ms. Noraiza Ismail, Education Dept.; Ms. Nicola Kuok, Puan Ros Mahwati Ahmad Zakaria, Ms. Farah Nurdiana Azhar, Ms. Kiew Yeng Meng; Mr. Md Rezad Adnan, Ms. Rekha Verma, Puan Adline Abdul Ghani, Ms. Nurul Iman Rusli, Puan Rashidah Salim, Puan Khalijah Yahaya, Islamic Arts Museum Malaysia.

A special thank to IAMM Conservation Center staff who contributed in presenting the objects in their best conditions : Mr. Friedrich Zink, Tuan Haji Mohamed Razali bin Mohamed Zain, Mr. Lalith Kumar Pathak, Mr. Mukhtaruddin Musa, Ms. Lalitha a/p Thiagarajah, Mr. Amiruddin Hassan, Fauziah Hashim and Nor Haizan Haromshah.

Acknowledgements from the British Museum

This exhibition began its life as 'Writing Arabic', a small display in the British Museum which, with the support of the Karim Rida Said Foundation and the Heritage Lottery Fund, toured a number of museums in the United Kingdom. At the initiative of Alistair Duncan, Director of the Altajir Trust, and thanks to His Excellency Mr. Mohamed Mahdi Al Tajir, the exhibition expanded and, as Mightier than the Sword, it was held at the Ian Potter Museum of Art, Melbourne in March – May 2003. Thanks now to Syed Mohamad Albukhary, the exhibition has changed again and is greatly enhanced by the addition of objects from the collection of the Islamic Arts Museum. I am grateful to Syed Albukhary and Dr Heba Nayel Barakat and to Nicola Kuok for all their help in making this exhibition happen.

I am grateful to His Excellency Mr Mohamed Mahdi Al Tajir, Ahmed Moustafa, and the other lenders for allowing us to include their objects and to Nassar Mansour for the graphics of the Arabic calligraphy. Many people have helped in the organisation of the exhibition and the catalogue in its various stages : Carolyn Perry and Zelfa Hourani, and my colleagues at the British Museum in the departments of Asia, Coins and Medals and Conservation. In particular I would like to thank Robert Knox, Stephen Ruscoe, Sophie Sorrondegui, Maureen Theobald and Janet Larkin and the photographers John Williams, Kevin Lovelock and Stephen Dodd.

For writing the coin captions, Cecile Bresc and Vesta Curtis. For help with reading some of the calligraphic pages Manijeh Bayani-Wolpert and Nabil Saidi and to Colin Baker for useful advice on Qur'ans. For advice on the metalwork Rachel Ward and Sue La Niece. For reading the manuscript and for making many useful suggestions I am greatly indebted to Sheila Blair, Michael Macdonald, Sheila Canby and to my husband Charles Tripp.

بكل آية سعادة وبكل سورة سلامة وبكل جزو اجز [...]

اللهم ارزقنا بالالف الفة وبالبا بركة وبالتا توبة وبالثا [...]

[...]وبار بالجيم جملا وبالحا حكمة وبالخا خلا فا وبالدال

[...]وا وبالذال ذكا وبالرا رحمة وبالزا زلفة وبالسين سنا [...]

وبالشين شفا وبالصاد صدقا وبالضا ضيا وبالطا طها [...]

وبالظا ظفرا وبالعين علما وبالغين غنا وبالفا فلاحا [...]

القا قربة وبالها كناية وباللام لطفا وبالميم وعطة وبالنون [...]

A *doa'* or prayer inscribed at the end of an 18th century Malay Qur'an.

14

Foreword

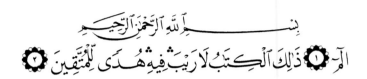

Alif Lam Mim, this is the Book; in it is guidance sure, without doubt, to those who fear Allah. (Surah Al Baqarah : 1, 2)

'*Alif*', the first letter of the Arabic alphabet is the module that regulates the size, shape and style for the succeeding letters. *Alif* becomes the keynote for the calligraphers throughout the Islamic dynasties. They contemplated its external and internal beauty and strived through Divine inspiration to reveal its' beautiful meanings. When these two components; Beauty and Meaning, were achieved the artefact radiates with energy and vivacity.

Mightier than the Sword exhibition showcases a selection of outstanding objects of art, which come from the rich collections of the British Museum and the Islamic Arts Museum Malaysia. The exhibition further contributes in highlighting the art of calligraphy in Southeast Asia and China. Furthermore, this cooperation aims at honouring the art of calligraphy in the Islamic world and strengthening the ties between both institutions.

Alif, Lam, Mim. It is through these mysterious letters of the chosen script and language, that the development of the art of Islamic calligraphy became flexible and ubiquitous. Islamic calligraphy developed different scripts to honour different texts, yet it was the meanings of the words that distinguished this Islamic culture from any other.

Syed Mokhtar Albukhary
Executive Chairman

Preface by
Syed Mohamad Albukhary

Allah,
provide us with each Alif fondness (Ulfa),
with each Baa blessing (Barakah),
with each Taa repentance (Tawba),
and with every Thaa reward (Thawab)...

This *doa'* or prayer inscribed at the end of an 18th century Malay Qur'an, attaches to every letter of the Arabic script a desirable trait. To the calligrapher the Arabic letters were instruments that contribute in the worshiping of Allah, the more they are written the more divine reward the calligrapher would achieve. With this approach the Arabic calligraphy was incorporated into the art objects elevating them in status to radiate blessings, beauty and meaning. When the script honours the text *barakah* (blessing) is achieved and in the process beauty and meaning become two sides of the same coin. This is when the pen becomes Mightier than the Sword.

'Mightier than the Sword, Arabic script: Beauty and Meaning' exhibition emerged under the auspices of the Islamic Arts Museum Malaysia and The British Museum through their collaborative efforts, in its new form. The travelling exhibition now incorporates over 100 artefacts from each collection and elaborates on the rise, development, spread and use of the script through showcasing exquisite inscribed objects from the earliest Islamic periods up to the present day.

Through contemplating these objects, it is our desire to train our eyes to see the invisible inner beauty of the Arabic script, to contemplate through the shapes of the letters to reveal the beauty that forms their soul.

The 16th century mystic calligrapher Babashad of Isfahan analysed the art of calligraphy into twelve components. He started by explaining the classical requirements of inking, composition, proportions, and the

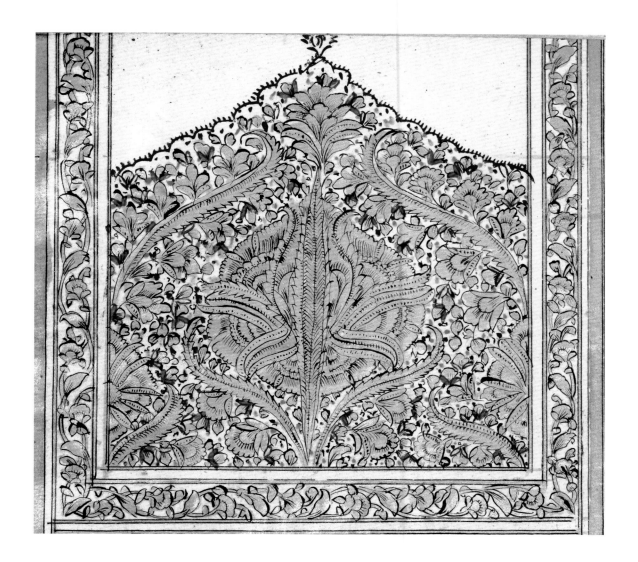

shapes of the strokes, but soon realised that it takes more than skill to produce wonderment. The last three components went beyond style and clarity, to the factors that elevate calligraphy beyond penmanship and render them in a masterly manner revealing the inner beauty of the Arabic script. These factors were purity; where the purity of writing is the outcome of the purity of the heart, Divine contemplation, and authority which reflects the total submission to God. With these factors in mind, we invite viewers to contemplate the exhibition 'Mightier than the Sword' with a new appreciation.

*"His **Alifs** were like the tall sapling figures that gives peace to the soul,*
*and the eye of his **sad** was like the eye of the youthful sweethearts.*
*His **dal** and **lam** were like the curls of heart-ravishing beloved,*
*And the circles of the **nun** were like the eyebrows of beauties.*
*Every one of his **dots** was like the pupil of the dark-eyed,*
*And every one of his **strokes** was like the water of life*
in the darkness of running ink."

Babahsad of Isfahan
1580 AD

قَالَ النَّبِىُّ عَلَيْهِ السَّلَام

فَقُلْتُ يَا جِبْرَئِيلُ مَنْ هُؤُلَاءِ قَالَ هُؤُلَاءِ أُمَّتُكَ الَّذِينَ يَقُولُونَ مَا لَا
يَفْعَلُونَ عَنْ مُعَاذِ بْنِ جَبَلٍ قَالَ سَمِعْتُ رَسُولَ اللهِ صَلَّى اللهُ عَلَيْهِ وَسَلَّمَ
يَقُولُ اللهُ تَعَالَى وَجَبَتْ مَحَبَّتِي لِلْمُتَحَابِّينَ فِيَّ وَالْمُتَجَالِسِينَ فِيَّ صَدَقَ اللهُ

Preface by Neil MacGregor

This exhibition celebrates the beauty of the word, of the Arabic word, sanctified by Islam and spread by adoption from West Africa to the Malay World. It is a word both intellectual and physical, where meaning and aesthetic play constantly together, intertwining, enriching and occasionally subverting each other. It was present at the beginning of the British Museum in 1753, for in the founding collection of Sir Hans Sloane, was a quartz amulet engraved with verses from the Qur'an and many of the objects discussed in this catalogue are from the British Museum's collection. They are complemented by works from the Islamic Arts Museum Malaysia made possible by this collaboration between our two institutions. They offer a glimpse of one of the great universal achievements of Islamic civilisation.

What is shown here is the word set free from the book. No longer narrative, it made its way into every area of human experience: verses of Persian love poetry on a tile, inscriptions on Mongol coins, an Afghan ewer or an axe from the Sudan; calligraphy by an artist living in the United Kingdom, or a 'calligraphiti' lithograph based on slogans scribbled on a wall in Gaza; the subtle adornment of an Iznik mosque lamp or the Cairo sticker of the 1990s protecting against the evil eye.

Trade ensured that the reach of Arabic calligraphy should not be limited to the Islamic world. The *shahadah*, the Profession of Faith that enlivens a Chinese bronze can also reappear in the unexpected setting of a Venetian painting, in the halo of Gentile da Fabriano's fifteenth-century Virgin from Pisa, quite legible and apparently quite theologically at home in its new Christian setting.

The training to become a calligrapher was long and demanding. It is no accident that two of the phrases most frequently set by master calligraphers to their pupils were: 'Oh Lord, make it easy and not difficult' followed by a phrase which even in un-aesthetic Roman type, may serve as the wish for this exhibition – 'Oh Lord may it be completed in the best way'.

Introduction

The transformation of the language
Narrated by Aisha the wife of the Prophet Muhammad SAW:[1]

The angel came to the Prophet and asked him to read - Iqra'
The Prophet replied, 'I do not know how to read.' The Prophet added,
'The angel caught me (forcefully) and pressed me so hard that I could
not bear it anymore. He then released me and again asked me to read,
and I replied, I do not know how to read,' Whereupon he caught me
again and pressed me a second time. He then released me and asked
me again to read, but again I replied, 'I do not know how to read (or,
what shall I read?)' Thereupon he caught me for the third time and
pressed me and then released me and said:
>   *"Read: In the Name of your Lord,*
>   *Who has created (all that exists).*
>   *Has created man from a clot*
>   *Read and Your Lord is Most Generous*
>   *He, who teacheth by the pen,*
>   *teacheth man that which he knew not."*

When the archangel approached Prophet Muhammad SAW and commanded him to read, it was also a command to be observed by the followers of Islam for the subsequent years. For centuries, the Arabic language—indigenous to the Arabian region, thrived in a rich and well-developed oral culture. Speech, debate, poetry, oratory and prose were considered the veneer of the elite, and the mastery of the language was highly regarded among pre and post-Islamic Arabians. Thus adhering to the command to read brought about a complete transformation of the Arabic language from a language behest by oral tradition into a written and visual form.

Prophet Muhammad SAW rose from this cultural climate as an illiterate Prophet as the Qur'an describes him, receiving the oral revelations of the Holy Words in the Arabic language.[2] After each revelation, the Prophet requested his scribes to quickly lay down the revealed words in writing, and to re-read them aloud to ensure the accuracy of the dictated messages. The Prophet understood early on the values of reading and writing. There were numerous opportunities to do so; one such example was during times of conquest when prisoners held captive were required to teach the Muslims the skills of reading and writing.

The encouragement given by Prophet Muhammad SAW to create copies of the Qur'anic *Surahs* brought special status to the scribes within the Arabic community. Furthermore, the Prophet and his companions praised not only writing but also writing in a beautiful and legible form, indicating that there was still room for development in pre-Islamic Arabic scripts.

When it was indicated to Prophet Muhammad SAW that his dictated messages, letters and treaties needed a written signature, he immediately ordered his seal to be engraved. The seal revealed three words: Allah, Rasul (messenger) and Muhammad SAW– one above the other.

The number of references found in the Holy Qur'an pointed to the importance of the transformation of the language from an oral to a written form. The Qur'an refers to the scripts as a written book (83:9, 20) and commanded all followers to read (2:44), and listen to the Holy Words when they are read out (7:204). The Qur'an directs Muslims to record their daily transactions, to reduce them to writing by directing a scribe to write and record them (2:282). Furthermore, it is mentioned that man's deeds were recorded (78:29) and his actions registered in books by the noble angels (83:11). There were also numerous references in the Qur'an that mention the Christians and Jews as the 'People of the Book' (3:70, 71).

With this special emphasis on the written form, calligraphy was elevated to a position of status and honour among Muslims. Islam further glorifies the position of the written form by requiring Muslims to be in a state of physical purification before they could touch the Holy Qur'an. The article by which this transformation was to be manifested is the Pen. The calligrapher's pen was particularly honoured in *Surah* 68 (The Pen) of the Qur'an: "*Nun and by the pen and by what it inscribes*". Similarly the pen was praised in *Surah Al Alaq* (96:4) "*Iqra'! And thy Lord is Most Bountiful, He who taught by the Pen*".

An Arabic Qur'an
The Arabic language was the language chosen to reveal the Qur'an. Consequently, it attained unique status in comparison to other languages and scripts of the time. The Holy Book mentioned the word Arabic ten times, emphasising the importance of revealing the Qur'an

in Arabic in the language of the common people (16; 103), and not in a foreign tongue. (41:44).

The Arabic alphabet contains seventeen characters, however with the addition of dots above and below the characters, they form twenty-eight distinct letters. It is noted that the earliest post-Islamic Arabic written on vellum, papyrus and gazelle parchments lacked such dotting system. It was during the times of the righteous Caliphs (632 – 661 AD) that the developed scripts, especially *kufic* evolved in time to incorporate the dotting systems, for reasons of clarity. The Arabic script further uses diagonal strokes and small characters above and below the letters to indicate sounds and stresses on vowels. Similar to the dots, the presence of these vocalisation marks were essential and mandatory for the reader. Although these characters may clarify the tense of a verb, or even change the meaning of a word, educated readers at present times do not feel the need for these units (tashkeel). As for the calligrapher, the aesthetic value of the Arabic letters, dots and strokes formed into three units that he could manipulate accordingly to create his beautiful works of art.

The Arabic script is written from right to left and exhibits letters that are horizontal and vertical, angular and curved. In a homogeneous and continuous manner, the letters may change their shape to adapt to the visually written word. With a combination of all of these factors, the Arabic script emerged to be a very flexible medium, aimed at achieving both balance and beauty. There were endless possibilities in manipulating the letters, and it became the calligraphers' noble aspiration to accentuate the beauty of the Arabic script.

Beauty and meaning
As the script developed, Arabic language was adapted as the administrative language under Caliph Abdul Malik Ibn Marwan (685-705 AD). The script transformed writing into a visible statement; creating an identity that united the Muslim world and spread the message of monotheism. The meaning of the words themselves became more important than the images and portraits of rulers found previously on coins and monuments. Calligraphy accordingly, replaced iconography to become epigraphs with beauty and significant meanings. It was the meanings of the words that distinguished this empire from any other.

Together the intrinsic beauty and meaning secured the Arabic calligraphy eternally in the arts of Islam. It ignited a spirit into a form, a soul into a character and provided the viewer with a state beyond worldly pleasure and aesthetic grace. Accordingly the Arabic language spread through time, place and media, to embellish every surface of objects, from the humblest to the most exquisite. And even when calligraphy was confined to stylised letters, repetitive blessings, and pseudo-writings, it was the script's divine connection to the chosen language that gave it pride and superiority above the other arts of Islam. Calligraphy as an art exhibited the principles of order and symmetry and through the understanding of the meaning of the words an expression of unity and reality is manifested, producing inner beauty in the process.

An excerpt from the writings of the eminent historian Khwanda Mir (d. 1535 AD)[3]

"The delight the human spirit derives from depictions and calligraphy, which is the lot of princes and viziers, rich and poor alike, cannot be put into words. And it is impossible to describe even a grain of the beauty, joy and rapture that rare art imparts through the brush and fingers".

"Every drop that the diver of the pearl-raining pen brings forth from the murky depth of the inkpot, to the shore of these folios is a priceless pearl and every picture that the artist of the mind has transferred from the tablet of the heart to the pages of this book is a light that delights the spirit."

The development of scripts

The earliest Arabic texts from the 7th century that exist today include single parchments of the Qur'an as well as several letters sent by the Prophet to foreign leaders. These two documents form an important beginning for the development of Arabic calligraphy. The content of these simple recorded words serve one clear purpose; an invitation to the concept of monotheism.

According to later historians, Prophet Muhammad SAW may have sent over forty letters to specific towns in Arabia, including tribal leaders and neighbouring rulers. The most known of which is a letter sent to Hercules, the Roman Emperor (Qaisar of Rum) in the 7th H/628 AD. The letter was written on vellum in *Madina* script, which includes seven lines of text, and culminates with the Prophet's seal. The letter, which is currently in the custody of the Hashemite family of Jordan, is written in a pre-*kufic* style with rigid angular letters, without dots and articulation marks. The script is characterised by its angularity and came to be known as the *Madina Hijazi* script.

Another style that developed in the Arabian region was the Mecca style also known as the Quraish style, characterised by its rounded form of letters. The Mecca style is evident in the letter sent by the Prophet, in the year 11th H/632 AD after reckoning the appearance of falsely prophets, and fearing for the consolidation of Islam.

The letter is perhaps sent to those regions where the falsely prophets persist. The letter is an order for the Muslims to slay the pretenders and maintain the true Islam. The letter was written on gazelle skin and can be found preserved at the Umayyad Mosque. Carbon dating and infrared photography proved the authenticity of the document and dated it to the Prophet's lifetime. The Prophet's seal ends the document, adding to the letter's authenticity.

The Caliph Othman ordered Zaid bin Thabit, Said bin Al-As, 'Abdullah bin Az-Zubair and 'Abdur-Rahman bin Al-Harith bin Hisham to compile the Qur'an in the form of a book (mushafs). Caliph Othman was recorded to say, "In case you disagree with Zaid bin Thabit (Al-Ansari; from Al Medina region) regarding any dialectic Arabic utterance of the Qur'an, then write it in the dialect of Quraish, for the Qur'an was revealed in this dialect."[4]

The second body of literature which sets the fundamentals of the written form of the Arabic language is the early Qur'anic parchments recorded and found in many of the Islamic libraries and provinces. Such parchments as well as complete copies of the Qur'an were a desirable acquisition even during the lifetime of the Prophet. Aisha, the Prophet's wife ordered Abu Yunus, a freed slave, to transcribe a copy of the Qur'an for her.[5] At the time when Caliph Uthman (644-656 AD) initiated writing an official version of the Qur'an and sent them to the major provinces, Hafsa's sheets were retrieved for verification. It is during this period that the pre-existing copies of the Qur'an should have been destroyed or the script removed. Accordingly old parchments with the Qur'anic verses, through modern equipment, show the traces of earlier script in the background. The re-using of parchments and papyrus paper was due to the scarcity of the material. Furthermore several artifacts inscribed with calligraphy appeared from the first century Hijra. An epitaph from the year 31H/652 AD and a tablet from 58 H/677 AD found on a dam with the name of Mu'awiya, reveal a very early stage of the Arabic script.

The first style to develop was the kufic where it evolved from the beginning of the 7th century AD by adhering to certain rules and distinct guidelines. The Qur'an remained to be transcribed in the kufic style up until the 4th century H/10th century AD. The kufic was adapted to different regions, and acquired the names of the geographical regions and dynasties. Eastern kufic and Maghribi kufic each presented a new embellishment. Ornamental kufic developed in different forms; letters were placed on an arabesque bed, vertical letters elongated, foliated, plaited, interlaced, intertwined, with some letters taking the form of animal heads and geometric knotting. The degree to which imaginations were exercised was beyond doubt overwhelming in its application.

However transcribing and copying of the Qur'an necessitated a flexible and speedy form of writing where accuracy and legibility were also the main concern. During this stage a hybrid script evolved which forced vizier Ibn Muqla (4th/11th AD) to codify the script according to strict measurements, points, and relationships. Ibn Muqla, followed by Ibn Al Bawwab created a systematic analysis of the Arabic letters; resulting in the identification of six different prevailing styles. Nevertheless the door for further innovations and development of the script were kept wide open. In due time, the cursive writing–of high prestige during this era of the Islamic world, developed to emphasise its roundness, curvatures and flexibility.

Calligraphers all around the Islamic world recalled the saying of the Prophet, *"He who writes in beautiful script the words 'In the name of God, the Compassionate, the Merciful' will enter Paradise without reckoning."* They also recollected the saying of the fourth righteous Caliph, Ali Ibn Abi Talib: *"Learn good writing O educated man, for writing is nothing if not an embellishment for the educated person, if you have wealth, your writing is an ornament, if you are needy it is the best livelihood."* To the calligrapher, serving God through writing in a wonderful manner secures the blessing in this world and the hereafter.

When calligrapher Mohammed Muhsin of Herat compiled a *Muraqqa'* (an album) of beautiful calligraphy in 1582 AD, he wrote in its preface:
"What an album,
Every page of which is a charmer
With a hundred hearts it pulls.
Its pages are models of paradise;
Its works are kneaded with ambergris
Every line of poetry in it has a unique charm,
Stealing the realm of the heart and soul
The images in it are sheltered behind veils,
Revealing the colours of pampered beauties" [6]

Likewise, the Mightier than the Sword album seeks to provide a royal treat and ultimate pleasure possible through beautiful art to its viewers. It joins in the eternal quest to present beauty and meaning in an art that emerged and developed while aspiring to reach the grandiose beauty of the very meanings it inscribes; the meanings of the Word of God.

1. Sahih Al Bukhari, *Volume 9, Book 87, Number 111*
2. Sahih Al Bukhari, *Volume 3, Book 31, Number 137:* The Prophet said, "We are an illiterate nation; we neither write, nor know accounts. The month is like this and this, i.e. sometimes of 29 days and sometimes of thirty days." Narrated by Ibn Umar.
3. Qazini,M.M. and L. Bouvat, "Deux documents inedits relatifs a Behzad, Revue du monde muslaman 26 (1914): 146-61.
4. Sahih Al Bukhari, *Volume 6, Book 61, Number 507:* Narrated Anas bin Malik:
5. Ibid, *Book 004, Number 1316:*
6. Thackston, Wheeler. Album prefaces and other documents on the history of Calligraphers and painters 2001, p. 36.

Islam and the Word of God

The origin and role of the Arabic Script

Until the 6th century, Arabic was a spoken language only. It was the language of Arab tribal kingdoms that had been established in central Arabia, southern Iraq and Syria many centuries previously. A sophisticated tradition of oral poetry grew up at their courts, handed down over several hundred years but only written down from about the 8th century.

Writing in the Arabic script was known among these communities for about 150 years before the advent of Islam, but only a few examples, inscribed on stone, have so far been discovered, at sites in Syria and Jordan. The alphabet used to write Arabic from the 6th century to the present day is a form of Aramaic script that belongs to the family of Semitic scripts. Aramaic had been used by the Persians as the official language of the western part of their empire between the 6th and 4th century BC in north-west and eastern Arabia. With Alexander the Great's conquest of the region at the end of the 4th century BC, Greek became the language of Government, but Aramaic continued to be spoken and written in everyday life, and is still spoken today in some parts of Syria. The Nabateans (whose powerful kingdom, based at Petra in Jordan, flourished from about 100 BC to 106 AD and stretched from southern Syria to north-west Arabia) wrote in Aramaic and the version of the script they developed came to be widely used throughout the region. In the centuries following the end of the Nabatean kingdom, the Arabs in Syria and Jordan and probably those who had settled in southern Iraq gradually started using the Nabatean Aramaic script to write their spoken language, Arabic. Scholars have traced the transition and development from Nabatean Aramaic to Arabic through a number of key inscriptions on stone in this region, from a beginning of Arabic language in Nabatean script in the early 4th century AD to Arabic language and script by the mid 6th century AD. [1]

It was the revelation of Islam in the 7th century that was to change dramatically the role of the Arabic script. For there was now a pressing need to write down God's words to the Prophet Muhammad SAW.

Proclaim in the name of your Lord and Cherisher who created, created man out of a mere clot of congealed blood. Proclaim and your Lord is most bountiful. He who taught by the pen, taught man that which he knew not.
Qur'an 96:4-5

The examples of the Qur'an in this section are from several different periods. The single page inscribed, in the majestic angular *kufic* script typical of early Qur'ans (Cat. no. 1), comes from the 9th-10th century. The Qur'an section (Cat. no. 2) in the simple, elegant, cursive *muhaqqaq* script favoured later, was copied in the 14th century.

Furthermore, single folios of the Qur'an demonstrate the various types of scripts as *maghribi* (Cat. no. 10) and *bihari* (Cat. no. 11). Full Qur'an copies express the exquisite illumination of their frontispieces. (Cat. no. 9). An interesting addition is the full Qur'an inscribed on canvas produced in 1738 AD. (Cat. no. 14) All of these examples demonstrate the vitality of the written words of God.

Watermark on hand made paper indicates the date and the manufacture company of the folios.

بالحق وما قلوا

ا انا ا لله ا فكا

حكماه و

لصلا

ولا موله و يو ه

كلهم يسهد

واد لكر ما

كهم طا

و ا لصح ههه

و ا احكا

و قد هو ا

1.
Qur'an page, black ink on parchment,
probably Iraq 9th-10th century.
15.6 cm x 23.40 cm
BM. 2001,0605.1

The text, inscribed in the angular *kufic* script, is from Qur'an chapter 4, from the end of Verse 157 to the beginning of Verse 161, written on parchment in brownish-black ink in eleven lines in the oblong format characteristic of early Qur'ans. The device of using red dots to aid with vocalization to distinguish letters of the same shape is seen here, while a cluster of gold dots marks the end of Verse 160. While the style of script was originally associated with the town of Kufa in Iraq and hence its name, *kufic*, it is clear that this style was practised in a number of centres in the central Islamic lands. [1]

1. Whelan 1990; Deroche 1992.
VP

32

2.
Ceramic mosque lamp
painted in blue and white,
Iznik, Ottoman Turkey,
c.1510.
27.8 cm (height)
BM.1983. 5 Godman
Bequest

God is the Light of the heavens and the earth;
the likeness of his Light is as a wick-holder
Wherein is a Light
(the Light in a glass,
the glass as it were a glittering star)
kindled from a blessed tree
(Qur'an 24:35-6)

In Ottoman Turkey, mosque lamps that hung from the ceiling by chains had more of a symbolic than practical function. Their shape was based on earlier glass examples from Mamluk Egypt (1250-1517) which provided light by means of a wick placed in a container of oil within the lamp.[1] This example, made at the potteries of Iznik in Turkey,[2] is decorated in the designs and colour scheme influenced by Chinese porcelain that was popular at the Ottoman court at this time.

The inscriptions in cartouches around the lamp in a combination of cursive scripts bear no relation to the function of the lamp. On the base in a cartouche are the words : 'Allah, Muhammad SAW, Ali'. (God, the Prophet Muhammad SAW and Ali, fourth of the 'Orthodox caliphs' and the first of the Shi'a Imams.) The other inscriptions are in *naskh* but cannot be deciphered.

1. Blair and Bloom 1997: 280
2. Atasoy and Raby 1989: 41, 94.
VP

Islam and the Word of God

33

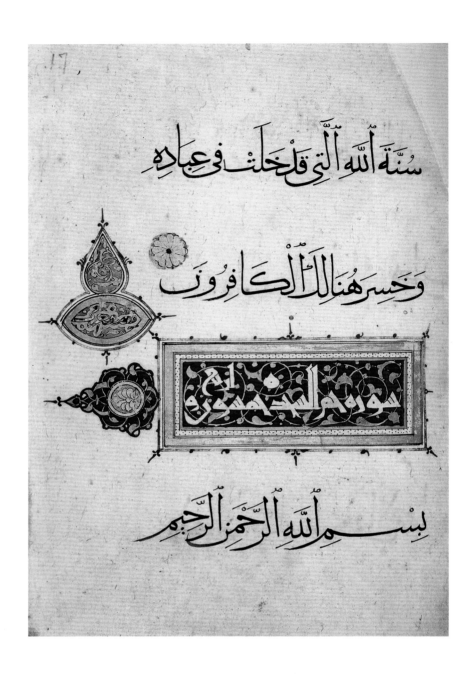

3.
Surah Al-Mu'min (the believer) and *Surah Ha Mim* also known as *Fussilat* (Qur'an chapters 40 and 41).
26.5 cm x 18.5 cm
Collection of H.E.
Muhamed Mahdi Al Tajir

This is part twenty-four of a Qur'an in thirty volumes (*juz'*) copied in *muhaqqaq* script in 14th century Mamluk Egypt, the main script favoured for copying the Qur'an in the Mamluk era.[1] The page on the left consists of the end of Chapter 40 and the beginning of Chapter 41. The name of the chapter is inscribed in white against a blue and gold ground in eastern *kufic* style, a variant of the *kufic* seen in cat.no.1. This style had been developed for the copying of Qur'ans in the 10th century but by this time had a mainly decorative function providing an elegant contrast to the simplicity of the *muhaqqaq* script.The end of the verse is marked by a gold rosette. To the left of it are a series of medallions of different shapes. In the centre of the oval medallion are the words *nisf* and *hizb*. *Nisf*, meaning half, indicates that this is the half-way point in part twenty-four of the Qur'an, while *hizb* means the sixtieth part of the whole Qur'an, which is the point that has been reached here.

1.Lings and Safadi 1976: 55 no. 78; James 1988 for Mamluk Qur'ans in general
VP

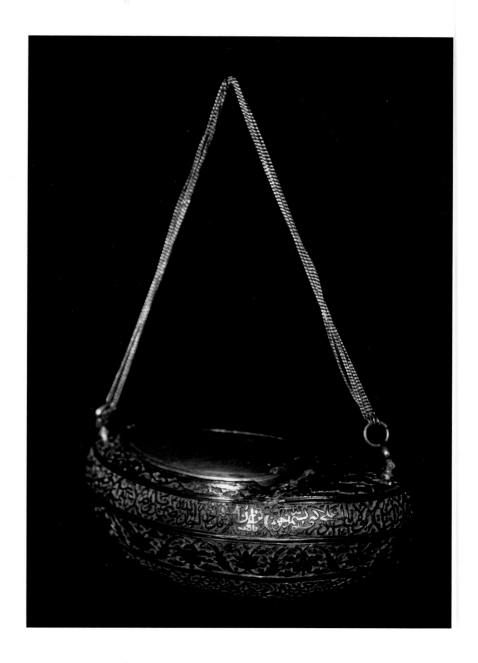

4.
Carved sea shell dervish bowl (*Kashkul*)
Safavid Iran, 1257 H/1841 AD
12 cm x 25 cm
2000.1.17

The dervish bowl has the shape of a half a coco-de-mer nut. A silver mouthpiece, lid and a hanging chain were added to the body presumably at a later period. The body is divided into three rows, the upper and lower containing inscriptions and the middle panel is decorated with a continuous row of floral scrolls. The base of the bowl is decorated with an elongated medallion reminiscent to those found on bookbinding.

Elegant simple *thuluth* inscription verses placed within lobed cartouches adorn the *kashkul*. The upper row contains the verses of *Surah Al Ikhlas*: The Purity of Faith as well as three pleas to God: "the loving and compassionate, the generous provider and the forgiver of all sins". These descriptions are used to call upon God, and they became popular in Iran,

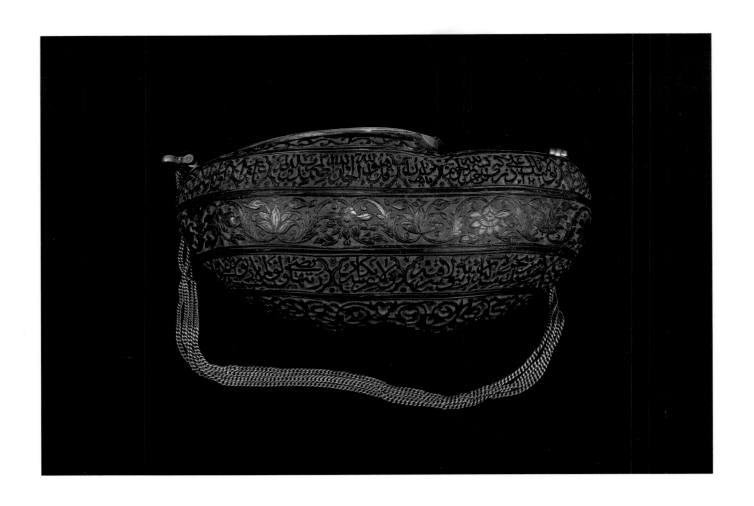

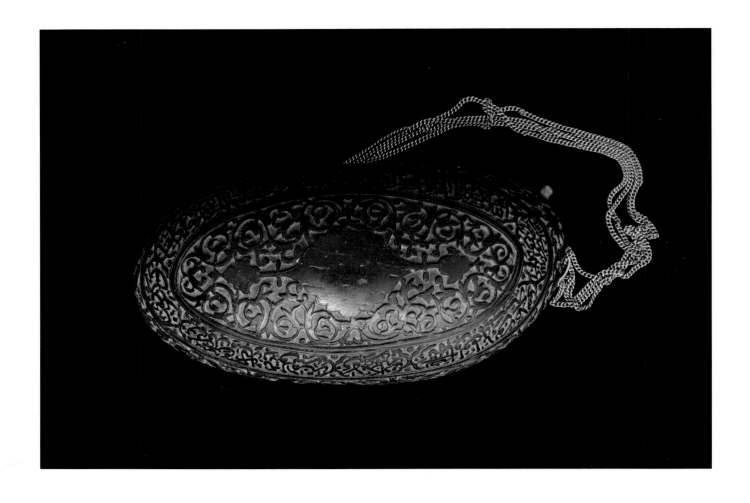

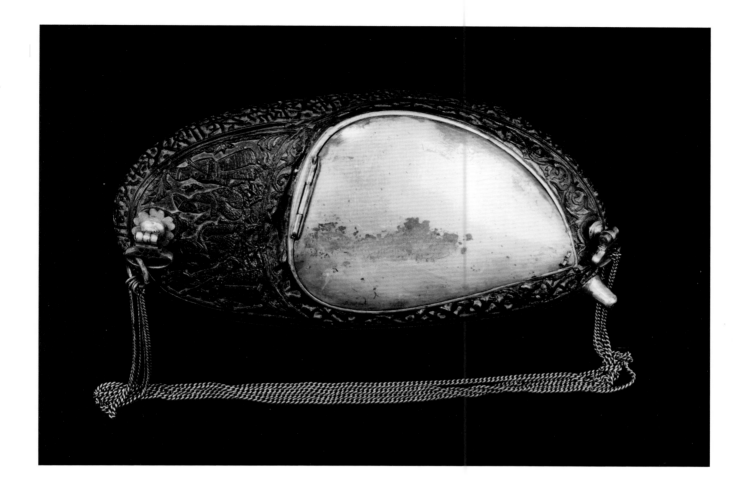

Central Asia and Ottoman Turkey during the 18th and 19th centuries. The upper frieze also contains the date of 1257 H which is equivalent to 1841 AD. A Shi'ah prayer in praise of Caliph Ali proclaims the *kashkul* as the product of Safavid Iran: *"Call for Ali the creator of miracles, you'll find him a help in time of trouble, all the worries and fear will disappear with you Ali, Ali, Ali".*

The lower row contains verses from the *Surah Al Nur*: The Light 24:35:

> *"God is the light of the heavens and the earth. The Parable of light is as if there were a Niche and within it a lamp: the lamp enclosed in Glass: the glass as it were a brilliant star: lit from a blessed tree an Olive, neither of the east nor of the west, whose oil is well nigh luminous, though fire scarce touched it: light upon Light! God doth guide whom He will to His light: God doth set forth Parables for men : a God doth know all things."*

On the top of the bowl, next to the covered lid an attendant is depicted sitting in front of an aged dervish, while two other attendants stand to their side, each holding a *kashkul* in his hand. Another *kashkul* lies in the background. The dervish and the younger attendants are all wearing a cone shaped headgear.

On the base of the bowl is an elongated medallion with arabesque scrolls surrounding it.

References:
Melikian-Chirvani, 1982, pp. 263-292
Melikian – Chirvani, 1991, p. 3-57
HB

5.
A woven silk panel
Safavid Iran, 17th century
44.5 cm x 90 cm
2002.10.15

A composition of an eight-sided star flanked by stylised tulips, trefoils and petals, forms the repeated unit of decoration on the buff coloured silk panel. The design gracefully incorporates calligraphic phrases within its units. The eight sided star recalls the words "*ya dayan* (the lender), *ya burhan* (the evidence)" alternatively with "*ya hannan* (the loving, the compassionate), *ya mannan* (the Generous Provider)" in mirror image compositions. The four words are a plea by which one calls upon God. The stylised leaf petal is inscribed with the phrase "Oh the innocent Imam", referring to the fourth righteous Caliph Ali Ibn Ali Talib. The pattern repeats every 50 cm length.

The merging of calligraphy, floral and geometric patterns gave way to outstanding compositions that were particularly suitable for religious use. A tomb cover from the shrine of Imam Riza at Mashhad, produced by Mir Nizam at Rasht in 1545, similarly recalls the plea to God, Ali and Muhammad SAW.
HB

6.
Fragmentary stone-paste commemorative tile panel, Iran second half 13th century.
81.0 cm x 56.5 cm
BM.1983.484 Godman Bequest

In medieval Iran, the deceased were sometimes commemorated on tile panels that were inserted into the walls of shrines. These panels, with the arch in the centre, also served as *mihrabs*. In this example,[1] painted over a cobalt glaze in gold and red, in a style known as *lajvardina* (from *lajvard* the Persian for lapis lazuli and cobalt), the inscriptions - *naskh* for the most part, with a single line above the arch in *kufic* - are moulded in relief. Around the panel, starting on the bottom right, is a verse from *Surah 41:30-1: 'Those who have said, 'Our Lord is God.' Then have gone straight, upon them the angels descend, saying 'Fear not, neither sorrow; rejoice in Paradise that you were promised. We are your friends in the present life and in the world to come; therein you shall have all that your souls desire, and all that you call for'.*

The incomplete *kufic* inscription has the words 'the only, the victorious', two of 'the beautiful names of God' which occur in the Qur'an. Under the lobed arch is the name of the deceased Jalal Al-Din Ismail, with his titles and the names of his forebears.

1. Porter 1995: 40
VP

7.
A set of 16 tiles
Morocco, North Africa
c. 14 century
9.5 cm x 9.5 cm
2002.2.125

A set of 4 rows of tiles, each comprising 4 tiles had once adorned a religious structure in Almohad Morocco. The red earth tiles are covered with a white slip ground before another layer of manganese glaze is added. The manganese is cut away leaving the calligraphy embossing and revealing the whitened ground. The calligraphy is rendered in simple *naskh* script, placed within cartouches, and the background is adorned with continuous arabesque leaves and scrolls. The first line reads: *"No power nor might without Allah, the Most High, the Incomparably Great".* The following lines similarly recall popular phrases from the Qur'an related to God granting help and victory to the believers, culminating with the phrase: *"Sufficient is Allah for us and he is the ultimate Trustee",* a section of *Surah* 3: 173.

These phrases are usually inscribed on tombs and rendered in the foliated *thuluth* script. The *thuluth* script developed in North Africa, was known as the Andalusian style. Similar examples can be found in stucco on columns from the Madrassah Al Attarin of Fez, (1325 AD), and Bu Inaniyyah Madrassah in Meknes (1358 AD).
HB

8.
**Marble frieze with Qur'an
verse inlaid with cinnabar
lacquer**
Mughal India
c. 17th/18th century
10 cm x 39 cm
2000. 2. 14

A raised white marble inscription frieze framed within a simple pointed arched cartouche, creating a vivid contrast against the red background. The inscription is in the *riqqa'* style, written during Mughal times (1526-1858), and reads: *"with him and there is no enemy but…"* The carved frieze is filled with a paste which is a type of lacquer, native to India, Burma and Southeast Asia, called cinnabar lacquer. This material is a red gummy substance deposited on the bank of certain trees by an insect (Coccus Lacca). This insect produces the waxy substance in its soft form, when collected the additives change its colour to either red or black.

Imperial Mughal architecture was characterised by another decorative technique, namely *pietra dura*, where stones were inlaid in white marble. This panel may be seen as the non-royal alternative to *pietra dura.*
HB

9.
Ottoman bound Qur'an
Turkey and N. India
1241 H/1824 AD
12 cm x 13 cm x 6.5 cm
2000.1.2

Handwritten in *naskh* script, the highly ornate Qur'an includes 24 pages of exquisite illuminations rendered on off-white burnished paper. The Qur'an manuscript begins with a double frontispiece decorated with a central medallion and axial pendants, inscribed in white *naskh* script against a golden background. The folio is then totally covered with an array of bright red rosettes, blue leaves and gold stems. The three pages that follow the frontispiece relate to pronunciation rules and explanation marks. The *Unwan* of this section is highly decorated with a huge golden lotus flower embraced by smaller stylised leaves. The script is in elegant *riqqa'* and these double pages have been refered to as carpet pages. [1]

A second double frontispiece appears in the subsequent pages. It hosts the opening *surah* of the Qur'an, *Surah Al Fatihah*. The double folios are highly illuminated with interwoven knotted bands in dark aquamarine, blue and bright gold rendered in the Kashmir style. All the *surahs* are written in simple *naskh*, while the *surah* headings are in *thuluth*.

The *Unwan* preceding *Surah Al Baqarah*; the second *surah* in the Qur'an, is similarly decorated with intricate interweaves of blue against gold, in the same spirit of the frontispieces.

Each page of the manuscript is divided into a field and a margin. The margin decoration consists of magnificent flowers and leaf branches. The leaves are in part framing notes and diacritic marks to assist in the pronunciation of the words.

There are two distinctly variant colophons at the end of the Qur'an. One contains guidance encircled by a medallion against a gold background, reminiscent to the *Doa* (prayer) page at the beginning of the Qur'an manuscript. The advice is attributed to Sheikh Al Jazari, Shams Al Din Abu Abd Allah Al Safawi and Abu Al Qasim Al Shatby. The second colophon indicates the date of the manuscript to be 1241 H or 1824 AD in a style popular during the reign of Sultan Selim II of Turkey (1774-1807).

The manuscript dates to two different periods with two different artistic styles.

The dense composition, which lacks European influence, suggests a northern Indian influence. The addition of illumination to existing manuscripts was a common practice among ateliers during the Islamic periods. Kashmir, where a similar dense style evolved is known to have revived a strong tradition of book production in the 18th and 19th century.

The manuscript is enclosed within a green Ottoman bookbinding and a green detachable leather case. Both are decorated with a stenciled bouquet of flowers, fashionable during 19th and 20th century Turkey.

1. IAMM lecture series 2004, Dr. Colin Baker.
HB

اعلم رحمك الله ان هذا المصحف المكرم مضبوط بالقراءات

العشرة فاما السبعة فعلى ما في الشاطبية والتيسير واما الثلاث

الزائدة على السبعة فعلى ما في الدرة والتحبير لابن الجزري رحمه الله

وقد وضعت الاساتذة علامات لاسامي القراء العشرة مع

رواتهم العشرين فقسموا الحروف الثمانية والعشرين لثمان عشر

رجلا وبقي اثنان مكان لهما اختلاف كثير ولم يبق لهما حرف

ابج	الامام نافع المدني	ب قالون	ج ورش
دهز	الامام ابن كثير المكي	هـ البزي	ز قنبل
حطى ح	الامام ابو عمرو البصري	ط ابو عمر الدوري	ابو شعيب السوسي
كلم ك	الامام ابن عامر الشامي	ل هشام	م ابن ذكوان
نصع ن	الامام عاصم الكوفي	ص ابو بكر شعبة	ع حفص
دصق ف	الامام حمزة الكوفي	ص خلف	ق خلاد

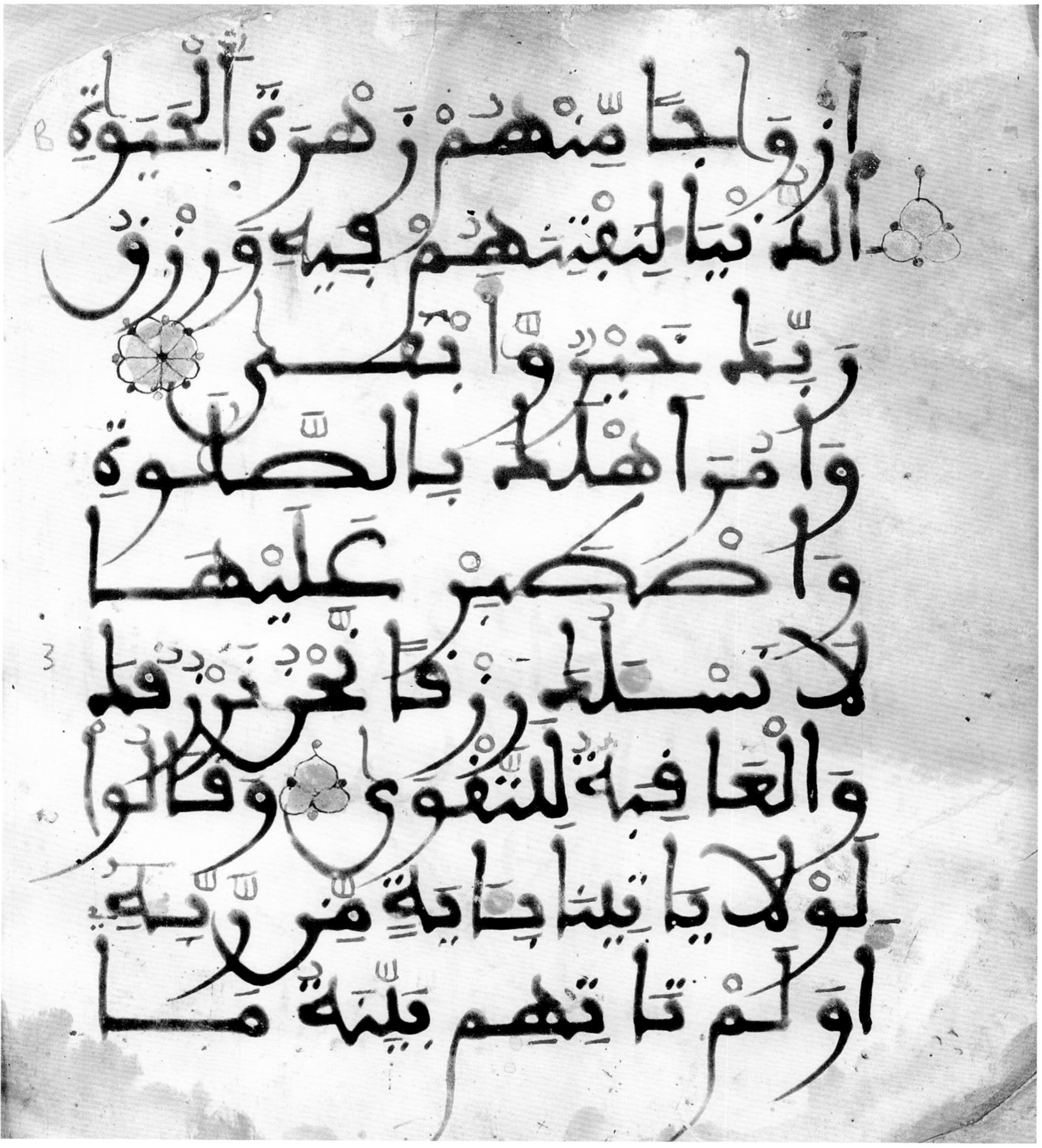

أزواجًا منهم زهرة الحيوة

الدنيا لنفتنهم فيه ورزق

ربك خير وأبقى

وأمر أهلك بالصلوة

واصطبر عليها

لا نسلك رزقًا نحن نرزقك

والعاقبة للتقوى وقالوا

لولا يأتينا بآية من ربه

أولم تأتهم بينة ما

10.
A double folio of a vellum
Qur'an
Andalusia, Spain
Early 13th century
23 cm x 21 cm
2001.1.158

The double folio reveals the final verses of the *Surah Ta Ha* inscribed in dark brown *maghribi* script on vellum. The folio, which exhibits nine lines of text per page, belongs to a large Andalusian Qur'an. The use of red, green and yellow diacritical marks, as well as blue and gold articulations enhances the calligraphy. Gold is also used to highlight particular words within and towards the end of the text.

The Andalusian style has its origins in Cordoba, and has attained its name after the generous patronage of Andalusian leaders of Spain. When it spread to Morocco it established close affinity with the Fasi Arabic script. Yet the true amalgamation of the scripts took place during the deportation of the Muslims from the Iberian peninsula. The final development of the North African style is known as the *maghribi* script.
HB

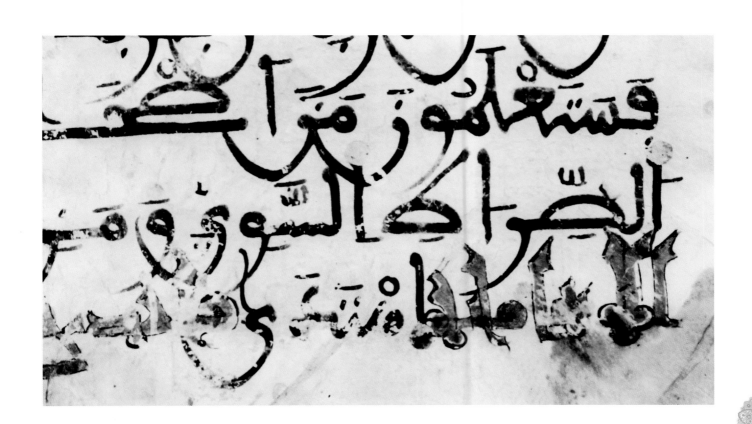

إليكم يٰبني آدم أن لا

تعبدوا الشيطٰن ط انه لكم

عدو مبين وان اعبدوني

هٰذا صرٰط مستقيم ولقد ط

اضل منكم جبلا كثيرا

أفلم تكونوا تعقلون هٰذه

جهنم التي كنتم توعدون

اصلوها اليوم بما كنتم تكفرون

اليوم نختم علٰى افواههم

وتكلمنا ايديهم وتشهد ارجلهم

بما كانوا يكسبون ولو نشاء

لطمسنا علٰى اعينهم فاستبقوا

الصرٰط فانٰى يبصرون

ولو نشاء لمسخنٰهم علٰى مكانتهم

فما استطٰعوا مضيا ولا يرجعون

11.
A *Bihari* style Qur'an leaf
Sultanate India
15th century
43 cm x 27 cm
2001.1.162

In deep black ink, the verses of *Surah Ya Sin* (*Surah* 36: 60-75), are written in *bihari* script with 15 lines of text per page. The word Allah is highlighted in gold, with recital marks in red and verse ending indicated with polychrome and gilt rosettes.

The *bihari* style developed and was used mainly in northeastern India and Afghanistan as a minor cursive script during the 14th and 15th centuries. The main characteristics of the script include extended horizontal uneven lines, thick round letters for emphasis and elongated, thickened and tapered ends of letters. Its letters are spaced so the open curves flow and a balance is achieved. This script is perhaps the earliest Arabic calligraphic style to be used in India prior to the Mughal period. Bihar was annexed to Delhi by Muhammad SAW b. Tughluk in 730 H/1330 AD. It belonged to Janunpur in 1397 and was held by the kings of Bengal until coming under the Mughal Empire.

Encyclopedia of Islam, new edition, volume 1 p. 1209 – Leiden, E.J.Brill, 1986.
HB

غَيْرَ الْأَرْضِ وَالسَّمَٰوَاتُ وَبَرَزُوا لِلَّهِ الْوَاحِدِ الْقَهَّارِ ۞ وَتَرَى الْمُجْرِمِينَ يَوْمَئِذٍ مُّقَرَّنِينَ فِي الْأَصْفَادِ ۞ سَرَابِيلُهُم مِّن قَطِرَانٍ وَتَغْشَىٰ وُجُوهَهُمُ النَّارُ ۞ لِيَجْزِيَ اللَّهُ كُلَّ نَفْسٍ مَّا كَسَبَتْ إِنَّ اللَّهَ سَرِيعُ الْحِسَابِ ۞ هَٰذَا بَلَاغٌ لِّلنَّاسِ وَلِيُنذَرُوا بِهِ وَلِيَعْلَمُوا أَنَّمَا هُوَ إِلَٰهٌ وَاحِدٌ وَلِيَذَّكَّرَ أُوْلُوا الْأَلْبَابِ ۞

سُورَةُ الْحِجْرِ سَبْعُونَ وَتِسْعُ آيَاتٍ بَابِ ...

بِسْمِ اللَّهِ الرَّحْمَٰنِ الرَّحِيمِ
الر تِلْكَ آيَاتُ الْكِتَابِ وَقُرْآنٍ مُّبِينٍ ۞ رُّبَمَا يَوَدُّ الَّذِينَ كَفَرُوا لَوْ كَانُوا مُسْلِمِينَ ۞ ذَرْهُمْ يَأْكُلُوا وَيَتَمَتَّعُوا وَيُلْهِهِمُ الْأَمَلُ فَسَوْفَ يَعْلَمُونَ ۞ وَمَا أَهْلَكْنَا مِن قَرْيَةٍ إِلَّا

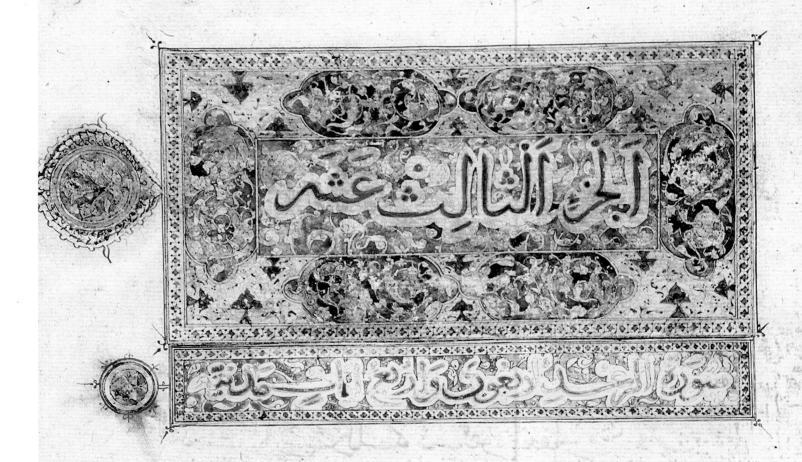

الجزء الثالث عشر

سورة الرعد بغوى وأربع الا أية مدنية

بِسْمِ اللَّهِ الرَّحْمَنِ الرَّحِيمِ

المر تِلْكَ آيَاتُ الْكِتَابِ وَالَّذِي أُنْزِلَ إِلَيْكَ مِنْ رَبِّكَ الْحَقُّ وَلَكِنَّ أَكْثَرَ النَّاسِ لَا يُؤْمِنُونَ ۞ اللَّهُ الَّذِي رَفَعَ السَّمَاوَاتِ بِغَيْرِ عَمَدٍ تَرَوْنَهَا ثُمَّ اسْتَوَى عَلَى الْعَرْشِ وَسَخَّرَ الشَّمْسَ وَالْقَمَرَ كُلٌّ يَجْرِي لِأَجَلٍ مُسَمًّى يُدَبِّرُ الْأَمْرَ يُفَصِّلُ الْآيَاتِ لَعَلَّكُمْ بِلِقَاءِ رَبِّكُمْ تُوقِنُونَ ۞ وَهُوَ الَّذِي مَدَّ الْأَرْضَ وَجَعَلَ فِيهَا رَوَاسِ

52

12.
Part 13 of a Mamluk Qur'an
Egypt & Syria
14th-15th century
55.4 cm x 39.6 cm x 1.5 cm
2003.6.23

The 13th *juz'* of a thirty volume Mamluk Qur'an was produced under the generous patronage of an ambitious amir. The full *juz'* is copied on 29 large folios. Each page hosts 11 lines written in a bold *muhaqqaq* script. *Muhaqqaq* means the meticulously produced script. It was favoured during the 13th and 14th centuries in Egypt and Syria.

The first folio displays a rectangular heading that is highly ornate. The decoration comprises cartouches filled with spiral arabesque scrolls, underneath which is the *surah* heading. *Surah* headings, common during the Mamluk period, were inscribed in the *naskh* script and placed within elongated rectangles ending with decorative roundels. Beautiful roundels and margin decorations adorn each page of the manuscript, their gold lustre against red and blue gives them a royal appeal. This *juz'* starts with *Surah Al Raa'd* .

The script creates a balanced contrast between the verticals and the elongated slanted horizontal letters. Mamluk Qur'ans are also charactarised by their large size. The 30 *juz'* would have been placed within a decorated wooden box before donating it as a charitable endowment. During the Mamluk period 30 *juz'* Qur'ans were sent to foreign rulers as royal gifts. Al Nasir Mohammed sent Oljaitu a set (1304-17) upon his conversion to Islam. Yet most of the royal Qur'ans were donated as waqfs for their respective foundations.

The outstanding margin decorations with superimposed geometric and floral decorations are typical to early *bahri* Mamluk Qur'ans. During this period side medallions radiate with energy as thin bands extended the composition that outline the pattern. During the 14th century the script inside the roundels changed from *kufic* to *naskh*. The *surah* headings within the *juz'* are written in the *naskh* script as well and are placed within simple decorative grounds.

1. Arberry (1967), p. 85 Mamluk Qur'an 14th century.
2. Atil, Washington, 1981. P.27
HB

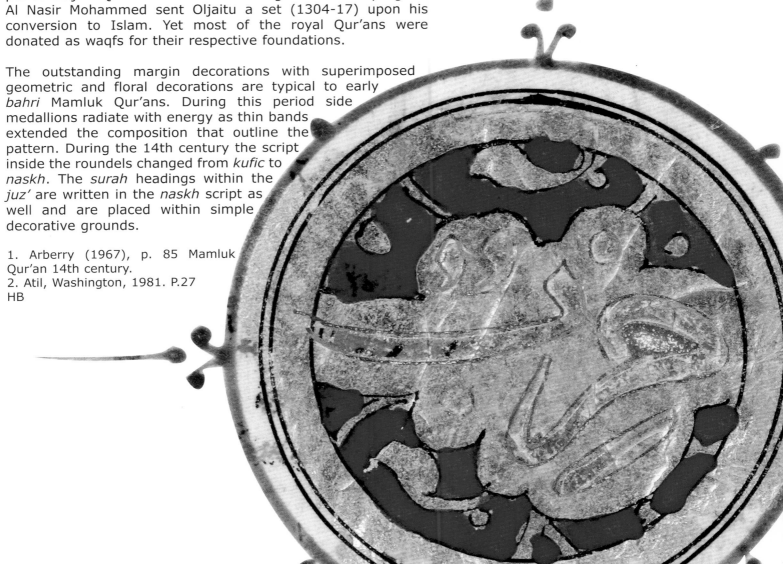

13.
Safavid Qur'an
Shiraz, Iran
16th/17th century
38 cm x 24.2 cm
2002.10.1

This outstanding complete Qur'an produced in Iran during the 16th-17th century exhibits within its 489 folios fine *muhaqqaq* script and *naskh surah* headings on outstanding illuminations. Two exquisite frontispieces adorn the first and second *surahs* of the Qur'an. *Surah Al Fatihah* is written in white against a dark blue oval medallion surrounded by Chinese cloud scrolls against a gold ground. At the end of the Qur'an manuscript are three illuminated end folios adorning the last *surahs* of the Qur'an. Between the verses are gold rosettes while illuminated marginal lozenges and stars adorn the edge of the folio, indicating the end of a section of the Qur'an. The main text is followed by a *falnamah* written as verses within smaller compartments.

The Safavid dynasty emerged in Iran at the turn of the 16th century as a strong power. Their ateliers depended heavily on the Turkmen and Timurid tradition and artistic styles. Yet soon generous patronage encouraged the development of several provincial centres of manuscript production. Shiraz emerged as a center with distinct style, elaborate illumination and outstanding calligraphy commissioned by the royal court. This Qur'an manuscript is the product of such ateliers.[1]

The following pages reveals the mastery craftmenship in Safavid Iran. The first frontispieces were carpet pieces to usher in viewers and to give illuminators the chance to express their talent.

1. James, Nour foundation, p. 184-189.
HB

فى كتاب مكنون

لا يمسه إلا المطهرون تنزيل من رب العالمين

إنه القرآن كريم

قال الله سبحانه وتعالى
والرحمن الرسول الحق
عليك بالقرآن مسد

لا يمسه الا المطهرون

فاتحة

وَإِيَّاكَ نَسْتَعِينُ اهْدِنَا الصِّرَاطَ

الْمُسْتَقِيمَ صِرَاطَ الَّذِينَ أَنْعَمْتَ عَلَيْهِمْ غَيْرِ

الْمَغْضُوبِ عَلَيْهِمْ وَلَا الضَّالِّينَ

آيَات

بِسْمِ اللَّهِ الرَّحْمَنِ الرَّحِيمِ

الٓمٓ ذَلِكَ الْكِتَابُ لَا رَيْبَ فِيهِ هُدًى لِّلْمُتَّقِينَ

الَّذِينَ يُؤْمِنُونَ بِالْغَيْبِ وَيُقِيمُونَ الصَّلَوٰةَ وَمِمَّا

رَزَقْنَاهُمْ يُنفِقُونَ وَالَّذِينَ يُؤْمِنُونَ بِمَا أُنزِلَ إِلَيْكَ

وَمَا أُنزِلَ مِن قَبْلِكَ وَبِالْآخِرَةِ هُمْ يُوقِنُونَ أُولَٰئِكَ

عَلَىٰ هُدًى مِّن رَّبِّهِمْ وَأُولَٰئِكَ هُمُ الْمُفْلِحُونَ إِنَّ الَّذِينَ

بسم الله الرحمن الرحيم

14.
Nadir Shah Qur'an on canvas
1150 H/1738 AD
India
246.5 cm x 144.5 cm
1998.2.335

An outstanding complete Qur'an written on canvas by the calligrapher Khwaja Mullah Nagsh Bijapuri, and illuminated by Muzayen and *Naqqash* Atiq Al Rahman Mudzalfet on the 5th of Ramadan 1150 H. According to the colophon, the full Qur'an was to be presented to Shah Nadir Shah, perhaps as tribute to a new ruler.

The Qur'an is inscribed in black *naskh* script on deep turmeric yellow ground. The center of the canvas is ornamented by a monumental band of green *thuluth* script recalling the first *surah* of the Qur'an; *Surah Al Fatihah*. The text is further ornamented by five *shamsahs* or decorative roundels, one at each corner and one at the center. The Qur'an is framed with a beautiful decorative boarder depicting outstanding vegetal and floral leaves and scrolls.

The calligrapher was apparently unfamiliar with the Arabic language, and accordingly made several mistakes that was scratched out and corrected throughout the text. He also abridged the central Qur'anic *surah* at the center by representing the beginning of two words as one syllabus. (the two words Al Ra-hman and Al Ra-him were represented by only one 'Al Ra' syllabus). This style was repeated several times indicating that the calligrapher chose to write or combine the words in that manner.

Complete Qur'ans written on canvas have been a popular art in small towns in the Indian subcontinent. The availability of large canvas became availabe in the market during the 17th and 18th centuries when European influence introduced large scale portraiture which became popular during the Qajar period. Similar Qur'ans were inscribed on green canvas commissioned by Amir Abdallah governor of Allahabad in 1720.

The calligrapher is from the town of Bijapur. During the second half of the 17th century Deccani language was developed as an amalgamation of Persian, Arabic and other local languages. This in turn can justify the abridgement of the Arabic letters, prevalent in the calligrapher's style. The Decanne dynasty came to an end in 1686 and Bijapur fell under the Mughal rule. Nadir Shah (1736-47) conquered several of these regions or was about to conquer them in 1736-38 AD.
HB

15.
Hand written Quran
Java, The Malay World
18th century
30 cm x 20 cm
2004.2.1

The complete handwritten Qur'an reveals the characteristics of the Southeast Asian manuscript decorations: long inward margins with three side arches each adorned with finials and wings. The colour schemes used are red, black and golden yellow. The text block of the frontispiece reveals designs springing from the surrounding nature such as pomegranate segments, large foliage and *Heliconia* flowers. The decoration of the frontispiece, back piece and central folio also resembles the traditional woodcarving and batik motifs.

The paper on which the manuscript is written is a European import, where watermarks reveal the words 'Propatria' and the image of a knight with a long stick, fighting a lion with a sword. This watermark is characteristic of a manufacturing house in Holland; Pieter Van der Ley, Dordreht, Amsterdam. The watermark changed and developed every year with a new batch of paper. This watermark belongs to the Garden of Holland produced between 1723-1727 AD. The paper attests to the trade between Europe and Southeast Asia. It also dates the manuscript to the first half of the 18th century.
HB

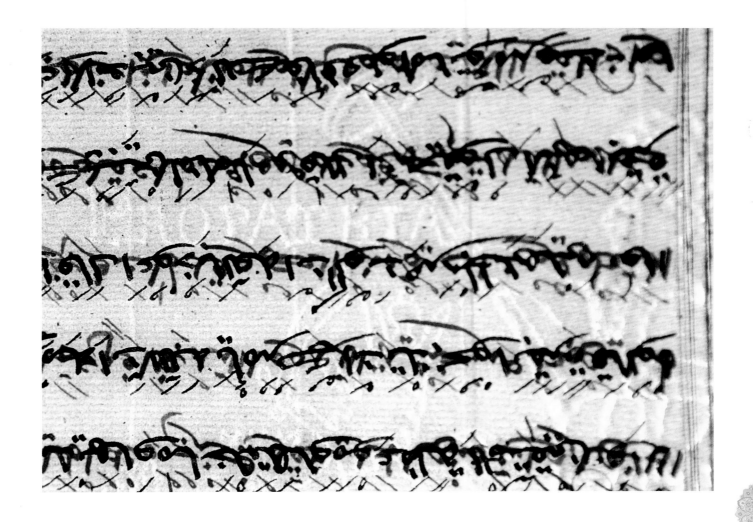

Beauty and Diversity

The development of the Arabic script

The defining feature of Islamic civilisation is the ubiquitous use of writing. There is writing from earliest Islamic times on everything from rocks in the desert (a tradition that had existed before the coming of Islam) to writing on architecture and works of art. The script began to be used very early as much for its decorative potential as for communication.

The most remarkable aspect of the Arabic script is its extraordinary flexibility, which allowed it to be written in a myriad of ways. This led over the centuries to constant creativity on the part of calligraphers, who perfected, embellished, re-invented and developed new styles. The establishment of Arabic as the language and script of the administration of the Muslim empire coincided with the recognition that in order to write the Qur'an, the most beautiful scripts possible had to be employed. Thus came into being a series of scripts developed by master calligraphers that were principally used for copying the Qur'an but were soon also employed in other contexts and media including secular texts, coins, gravestones, foundation inscriptions, tiles and so on.

Pre-eminent among the early scripts is *kufic*, so-called after the town of Kufa in Iraq. This script is characterised by elegant angular forms that were to vary widely in relation to time and place of production. It is in the first dateable Qur'anic inscription in *kufic* script, in the mosaics of the Dome of the Rock in Jerusalem built in 692, that in order to prevent misinterpretation of the words of God, the first attempts to distinguish letters of the same shape – by placing marks above or below letters of the same shape – can be clearly seen[1]. This was followed over the centuries by the appearance of a range of other scripts such as the *maghribi* script of North Africa from the 10th century, which elegantly combines the angular features of *kufic* with more rounded elements.[2]

By the 10th century, there were said to be at least twenty different cursive styles of script that had proliferated over the years, largely used for personal correspondence or to meet the needs of the bureaucrats and merchants. This was in contrast to the *kufic* script used to copy the Qur'an. Charged with the task of standardising and refining the myriad cursive scripts was the great calligrapher Muhammad SAW Ibn Muqla (died 940), a vizier at the court of three Abbasid caliphs. He and Ibn Al-Bawwab (died 1022), who was said to have been taught calligraphy by Ibn Muqla's daughter [3] after his death, established what are traditionally known as the 'six calligraphic styles', the *aqlam al-sitta*.

The problem with *kufic* was that while beautiful, it became ever more difficult to read as its decorative potential became increasingly exploited. This was compounded by the frequent lack of dots to distinguish letters, particularly on monumental inscriptions. The new system was based on a set of strict rules. The guiding principle was the use of a standard circle, a standard letter, *alif,* and a 'rhombic dot' (see p.226). This is described by Gaur as follows:

'The rhombic dot is formed by pressing the pen diagonally on paper so that the length of the dot's equal sides is the same as the width of the pen. The 'standard' alif is a vertical stroke measuring a specific number of 'rhombic dots'. The 'standard circle' has a diameter equal to the length of the standard alif and provides the proportional grid for all letters. Thus the various cursive styles are ultimately based on the width of the pen used by the scribe and the number of dots chosen to fashion the standard alif; these can be five to seven in number.' [4]

The advantage of this system was that it meant that the calligrapher could work in larger or smaller formats simply by varying the size of the nib. The letters would always be in proportion to one another.

The change from *kufic* to cursive scripts starts to be seen in monumental inscriptions on buildings from the 11th century. [5] By the 13th century, throughout the Islamic lands, the *kufic* script had been largely abandoned for general use, but had found other roles. It was henceforth reserved for particular types of religious inscriptions, such as the archaic prayer formulas on the brass ewer (Cat. no. 21) for example, for the Islamic Profession of Faith (*shahadah*) on coins, or for the chapter headings on Qur'an manuscripts (Cat. no. 3). In each case it provided a contrast of meaning and style to the inscriptions in *naskh*, *thuluth* or other cursive scripts. It also continued in some areas to be used in magical inscriptions as it was believed to be more powerful in the writing of charms.

Each of the six calligraphic styles (*naskh, thuluth, muhaqqaq, rayhan, tawqi' and riqa'*) developed for copying the Qur'an had particular characteristics (p.225) and different uses. The small-scale and neat *naskh* was often used for the copying of documents as well as Qur'ans and the larger scale and more formal *thuluth* was favoured by the Mamluk sultans of Egypt for its monumental and decorative qualities (Cat. no. 22). One of the greatest contributions of Persian calligraphers was *nasta'liq*, the 'hanging script', supposedly perfected by the calligrapher Mir Ali of Tabriz (died 1446) after dreaming of flying geese.[6] Particularly suitable for writing Persian, the structure of this poetic language with its frequent use of final letter *nuns* (n's) and *yas* (y's) lent itself to being exploited decoratively. This script predominates from the 16th century in Iran (Cat. no. 103) and then in Muslim India, and was even used by British officials serving in India. Other regions developed their own characteristic styles: the *sini* script of China, (Cat.no. 115) *divani* used by the chanceries of Ottoman Turkey and Safavid Iran (Cat. no. 88), *tughra'i* in states of Muslim India (Cat. no. 35), with additional virtuosi scripts used in specific contexts – the Ottoman *tughra* for example (Cat. no. 92) and zoomorphic scripts.

The objects grouped together in this section have several stories to tell, both in terms of the varieties of script with which they are inscribed, and what the individual inscriptions tell us about the context in which these objects were made. The shifting balance between communication and decoration can be clearly seen: at one end of the scale, the inscription is written simply, principally in order to communicate (for example, the coins and coin weights, or the Persian tiles, Cat. no. 25). Whereas the stark beauty of the *kufic* inscription on the Nishapur bowl (Cat. no. 16), or the dramatic *thuluth* 'flame script' inscriptions glorifying the sultan on the Mamluk brass tankard (Cat. no. 22) indicates that these inscriptions were intended to impress by their virtuosity, as well as to inform. The language used in this group of objects is generally Arabic, but there are examples of Persian on a tile (Cat. no. 26) and coins; Central Asian languages are used on Mongol coins (Cat. no.39).

On the back of a lacquered mirror, the physical description of the Prophet is complimented by its beautiful and serene presentation and as a single folio. (Cat. no.31) The Friday prayer scroll, made to be communicated with the audience, reflects the importance to present the text in a beautiful composition. (Cat. no.33) The different media; metal, marble, tiles and parchments, on which important phrases and verses were written, demonstrates the ubiquity of calligraphy.

1. Blair 1992: 59-87; Bloom and Blair 1997: 65
2. There is a vast literature on this subject. Some useful surveys are 'Khatt' and 'Kitaba' in the Encyclopaedia of Islam (New edition) vol. V; Guesdon and Vernay-Nouri 2001; Blair 1998; Safadi 1978.
3. Minorsky 1959: 56
4. Gaur 1994:90
5. Tabbaa 1994: 127
6. Minorsky 1959: 100; Safadi 1978:27

16.
Slip painted earthenware bowl, Nishapur or Samarqand, eastern Iran/Central Asia c. 9th-10th century
19.6 cm (diam.)
BM.1948,1009.02

The Arabic inscription in black angular *kufic* script, includes around the edge, the phrase 'Livelihood is distributed by God among people' and in the centre the word *Ahmad* which can mean 'more praiseworthy' as well as being a name. [1] The remarkable use of script on ceramics of this type, both as a way of conveying words of wisdom and for decorative purposes, has been linked to the aspirations of the ruling Samanid dynasty who were significant patrons of the arts and of literature. Many of the inscriptions on this group of ceramics consist of proverbs or wise sayings in Arabic and as such they are important literary documents. There was extensive ceramic production at both Nishapur and Samarqand (old Afrasiyab) producing a wide range of elegant table wares in addition to more functional pottery. [2]

1. Ghouchani 1986:182
2. Moulierac et. al 1992; Wilkinson 1973
VP

17.
Limestone tombstone,
Aswan, Egypt, 412/ 1021
64 cm x 49.5 cm x 16 cm
BM.1887,0402.1437

This is one of a large number of marble and limestone tombstones recorded from the cemeteries of Upper Egypt, other examples of which are in the British Museum.[1] The deceased is Fatima daughter of Ja'far, daughter of Muhammad Al-Sabbagh, (the dyer) who died in the month of Jumada II year 412 (September – October 1021) of the Islamic era. The inscription starts with the *basmalah* and continues with

Qur'an Chapter 112. God's blessings are then called on the Prophet Muhammad SAW and his family followed by the name of the deceased and the date she died. The style of the script is angular *kufic* but with flourishes at the ends of the letters that are characteristic of monumental script of this period. What is noticeable from the texts of the gravestone's inscriptions in this period is the increasing veneration of the Prophet's

family and the piety of women – as with this example, many of the tombstones recovered from Aswan are the gravestones of women.

1. Wright 1887: 332. There are others in the Petrie Museum, University of London. See also Hawary and Rached 1932-8 and Wiet 1936-42; Blair 1998: 196
VP

74

18.
Cast bronze round mirror
Khorasan, Iran
13th century
10.7 cm diameter
2003.6.4

The back of the mirror displays a moulded decorative composition of two winged lions with human heads turning to face the audience. A band of Arabic calligraphy in foliated *kufic* encircles the central composition, and invokes good fortune onto the owner. Foliated *kufic* is the earliest decorative script used in Islam, where foliage springs out of the ends of letters. The inscription is in a rhythmic form and includes the following words: *"Might and lasting life, good fortune and beauty, magnificence and praise, alacrity and elevation, possession and growth, to its owner forever."*

The iconography on the mirror springs out of the *mina'i* underglazed ceramics produced in and around the city of Rayy, Iran, during the 13th century. The split symmetrical trilobed floral motifs and the winged sphinxes commonly adorned such vessels. Similar mirrors have been used at a later period to host talismanic plaques, and in many cases they were cast by moulds using the available metal.

Similar mirrors are displayed in the Khalili collection (p.128), and Melikian-Chirvani, (1982), (p.130-131).
HB

19.
An engraved brass tray
Mamluk Egypt and Syria,
Early 14th century
61 cm diameter
2003.10.26

An outstanding round brass tray with raised rim depicting in low relief a series of four phrases of elongated *thuluth*. The inscription dates it to the period of Al Malik Al Nasir Ibn Qalaun (first quarter of the 14th century) where this style was in vogue.

The inscription can be deciphered as:

"The royal abode, the generous, the high, the lordly, the Emir, the refined, the learned, the diligent, the safe-keeper, the warrior, the defender, the victorious (Al Nasiri)."

The central medallion is composed of six small roundels engraved with seated figures representing the planets surrounding the central sun disc. The moon is represented as a figure holding a crescent, Mercury as a figure holding a scroll, Venus as a figure playing a lute, Mars as a figure holding a sword in action, while Jupiter and Saturn are figures holding a napkin in one hand. The appearance of the planets was common during the 13th and 14th centuries in the Islamic World.

The whirling rosette surrounded by a bird pattern was a known motif that can be found on the interior of bowls produced during the period of Sultan Al Nasir Muhammad SAW Ibn Qalaun (d. 1341).[1] Similarly, the horse rider with one hand raised is another typical motif that adorned early Mamluk metal works.

On the cavetto of the flattened rim are two emblems, one of a fleur-de-lis and the other of a harp intersecting a band of pseudo calligraphy presumably indicating a phrase wishing for perpetual glory to the Sultan.

The integration of symbols like the fleur-de-lis, which may have been introduced into Mamluk decorative art through their contact with the Crusaders, became a common trend towards the 14th century. Crusader prisoners were sent to Mamluk Damascus to work on construction projects, while stone workers were recruited in construction activities in Egypt. Similarly the influence of Mosul metalworkers was apparent in Mamluk ware since the second half of the 13th century where the surfaces became divided into roundels with huntsmen and zodiac signs.

The shallow carving and the stress on shapes rather than details indicate that another layer was to be added. Yet the lack of surviving silver inlay may be due to a job executed in haste, or due to its deprivation of the precious material by later owners, at a later period.

1. Ward, Rachel, Islamic Metalwork, the British Museum Press 1993, p. 112.
HB

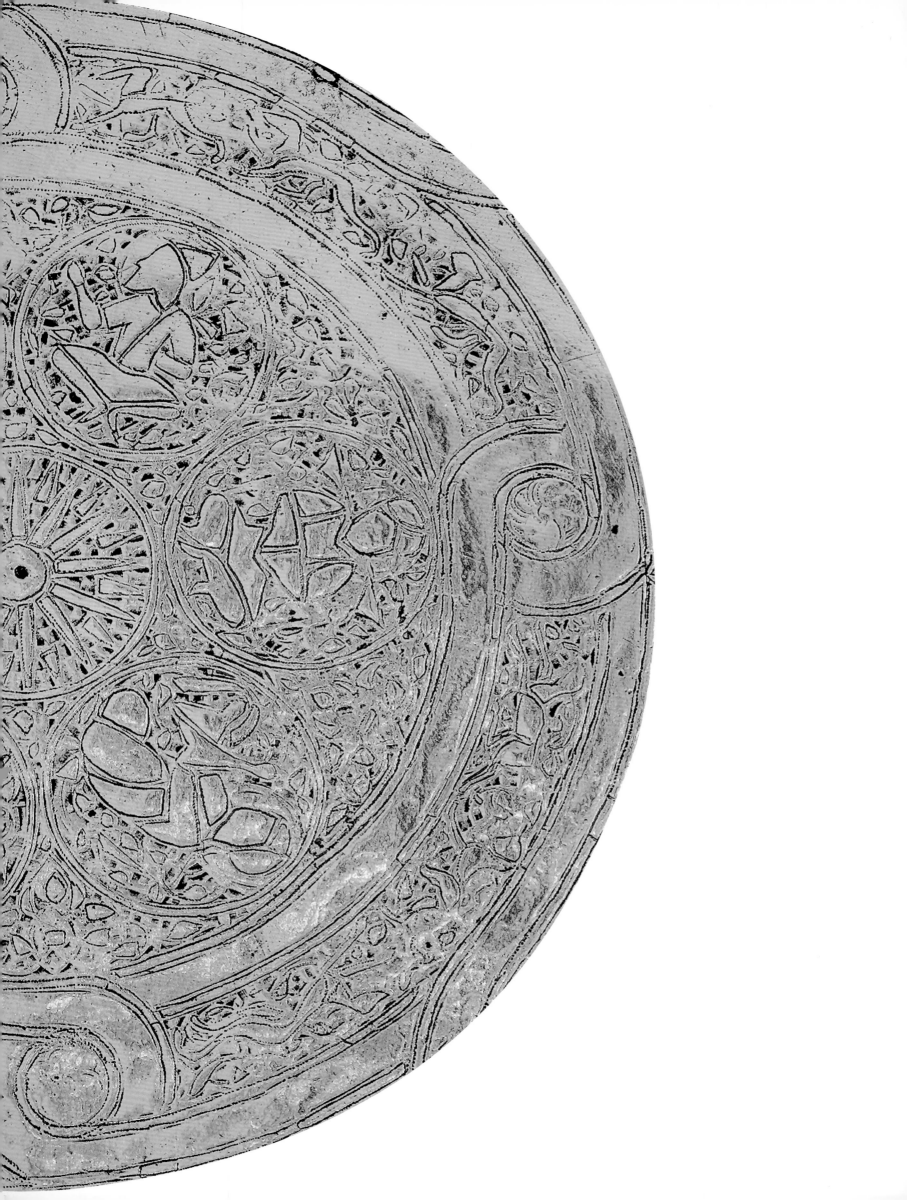

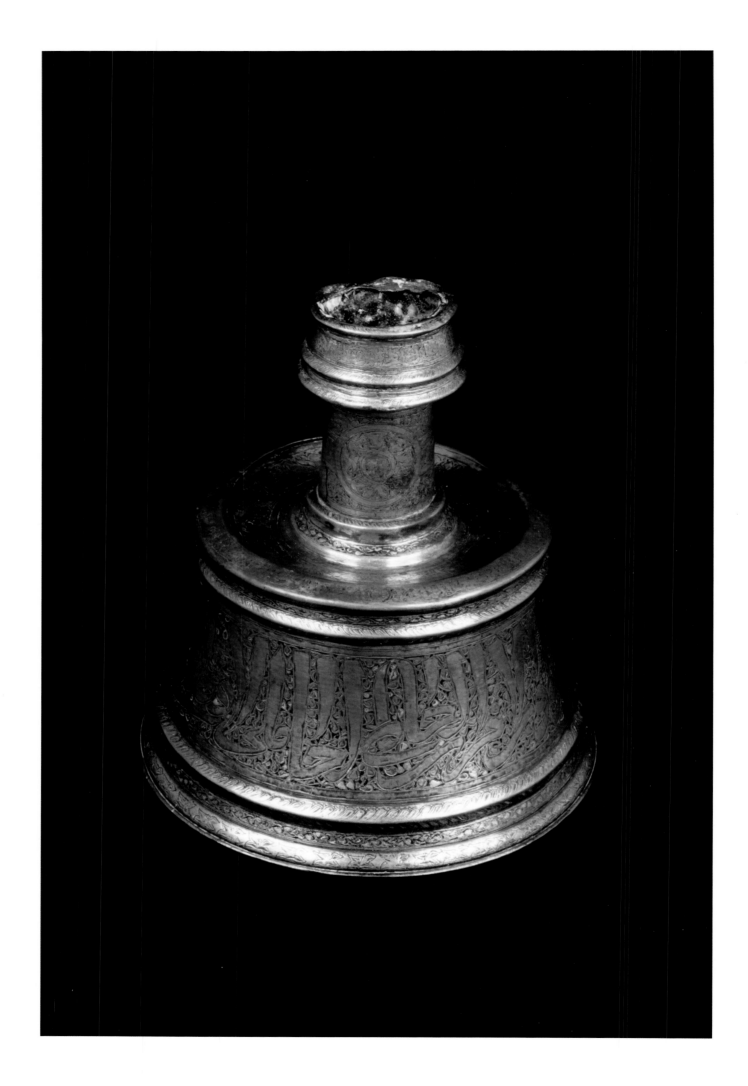

20.
Brass candle stand
Bahri Mamluk, Egypt or Syria
1293-1341 AD
20.5 cm x 19.5 cm
2001.1.205

Among the most impressive objects produced under the Mamluk patronage were a group of metal candle stands with elongated bold *thuluth* inscriptions. Technically the candlesticks were made of two sections, the neck and socket, and the shoulder. This brass candle stand has a typical Mamluk shape and is dated through the inscription to the reign of Al Nasir Muhammad Ibn Qalaun, (1293-1341), when numerous Mamluk emirs glorified their rank by placing their emblem (blazons) or dedications to their sultan on commissioned art works.

The bold *thuluth* inscription circles the main body of the shoulder. It is set against a simple floral design where a significant portion of its silver inlay has disappeared. Two braided protruding borders enclose and highlight the inscription band. The calligraphy states: *"The honourable authority, the high, the lordly, the emir, the learned, the diligent, the most excellent, the most perfect, the master, the possessor, (the officer of) Al- Malik Al Nasir".*

The socket contains a narrow faded band of inscription. The little letters still visible may be read as words glorifying the patron. The emblem on the neck contains bird like motifs surrounding a water wheel medallion. Another inscription band interrupted by small medallions with water wheel and swastika designs surrounds the rim of the shoulder. In time, the inscription whithered leaving slight traces of letters as well as two imposed phrases that have been added by a later owner. The decorative elements used in the candlestick such as the water wheel, the abstract floral backgrounds, the braided bands, and the hatching filled with bituminous material are all indications of a genuine Bahri Mamluk repertoire.

Mamluk candle stands were produced in large quantities for ceremonial processions such as the candlelit march, yet their main purpose was lighting and adorning the sides of the mihrab inside mosques. The Egyptian historian Al Maqrizi (H 767-846/1364-1442 AD) records that Sultan Al Malik Al Ashraf Khalil Ibn Qalaun ordered his vizier in 1293 AD to address Damascus with a request for one hundred copper candle stand, bearing the sultan's title. The Sultan also commissioned another one hundred sticks, fifty in gold and fifty in silver. (Al Maqrizi khitat Vol. II. P. 112)

The inscription placed on an abstract floral background, occupying a central position, is commonly found on objects commissioned during the period of Al Nasir Mohammed. But the origin of this style which is characterised by elongated vertical letters such as *"Alif and Lam"*, can be seen in the Mosul area during the Abbasid Caliphate. Although it is common in metal work during the Mamluk period, it was used at an earlier stage in Persia and was developed during the Il Khanid period (H 767-846/1364-1442 AD).
HB

21.
Brass ewer, inlaid with silver and copper, Herat, Afghanistan, late 12th- early 13th century.
38 cm (height)
BM.1848,0805.1

The ewer made of several sheets of brass hammered and welded, is remarkable for its extraordinary decoration and sophisticated metalworking techniques. Lions and birds stand out in relief on the shoulder and neck of the vessel. The inscriptions that form the main element of the inlaid decoration are all over the vessel. On the body they are in vertical bands of *kufic* and contrasting cursive *naskh* inscriptions. In *kufic* script is the dedication to an unnamed owner: '[May it belong] with bliss, divine grace, good fortune, immunity, divine solicitude, contentment, long life to its owner'. The inscription on the shoulder has rectangular pieces of silvers on the tops of the letters. On similar vessels of this period, these have faces etched into them. This ewer is one of a group of similar ewers made at Herat in the province of Khurasan in present-day Afghanistan. [1] An example in the Tiflis Museum is inscribed with a poem that shows the pride of the metalworker, what it was used for and where it was made :

'My beautiful ewer, pleasant and elegant

In the world of today who can find the like ? …..
This ewer is for water and they make it in Herat…..
Let happiness come to him if he gives the ewer to a friend.
Let trouble come if he surrenders it to an enemy'

1. Melikian-Chirvani
1982:16,114-8; Ward 1993: 76
VP

22.
Tankard of sheet brass
engraved and inlaid with
silver and gold,
Damascus or Cairo, late
14th century
28.5 cm (height)
1867,0612.1

The Arabic inscriptions in *thuluth* script with a band in stylised plaited *kufic*, are the main feature of the design. Repeated all over the vessel are words addressed to an unnamed sultan: Those around the body read: *'Glory to our Lord the Sultan, the King, the Wise, the Diligent,* *the Just, the Conqueror, the Holy Warrior, the Defender, the Protector of Frontiers, the One Fortified by God'.* The most striking aspect of the inscription is the elegant way in which the ends of the letters have been turned into exotic flames. There are other remarkable features: Within the densely decorated background are roundels, the one at the base of the handle featuring a delightful pattern of flying cranes. These and other designs such as the lotuses and peonies were largely inspired by Chinese textiles imported into the Islamic world at this time.

Ward 1993: 115
VP

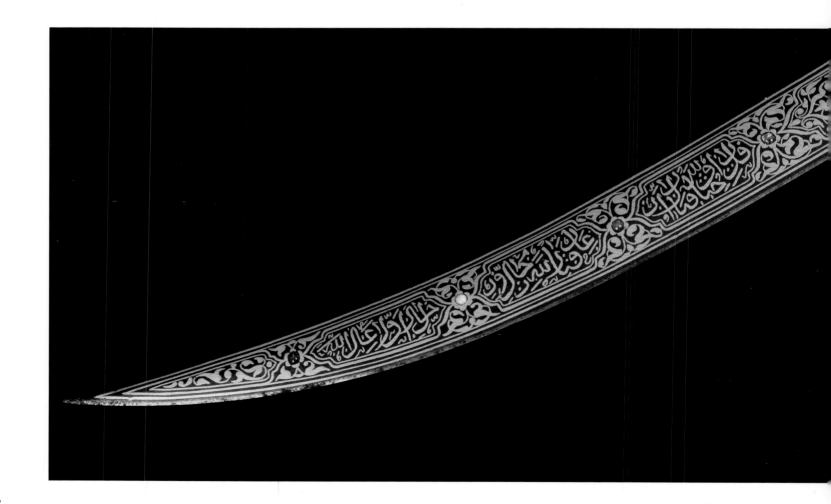

23.
An Ottoman dagger
Turkey
1098 H/1686 AD
Length 43.8 cm
2003.10.32

An elegant well proportioned steel dagger with jade handle and inscribed blade. The blade is engraved and has cartouches inscribed with Arabic phrases. Only the inscribed date and name of worker : Arif, 1098 H. were decipherable. The jade handle is finely inlaid with precious stones and coral. Such daggers would have served a ceremonial purpose where the decorative composition of the calligraphy was meant to be displayed. On the blade, in between the cartouches single semi precious stones were inserted.

HB

24.
Blue and turquoise
lustre tile
Kashan, Iran
13th–14th century
30 cm x 19.9 cm x 5.5 cm
2004.1.2

This star shaped octagonal tile contains a band of *naskh* inscription framing an interlaced arabesque design. The *naskh* border inscription band is inscribed with a poetic verse in Turkic – Persian script, recalling a *doa'* or prayer. The prayer calls upon God by the Arabic word "Rabana" our God, a phrase commonly used by Iranians of provincial Turkish dialect. The verses seek God's blessings,

sustenance and prosperity. Inscribed along the edges are four lines of the opening of Ferdowsi's Shahnameh, translated below. Aside from Shahnameh poetry, the rest of the star is inscribed with fragments of poetry belonging to other poets.

"In the name of the God of life and wisdom
The God of highest thought
The God of name and place

The God who gives us our bread and guides us"

Stylistically the tile is closely related to others which were lining the walls of the Imamzada at Qom (1334 AD).[1]

1. Watson, 1985, p.140-149.
HB

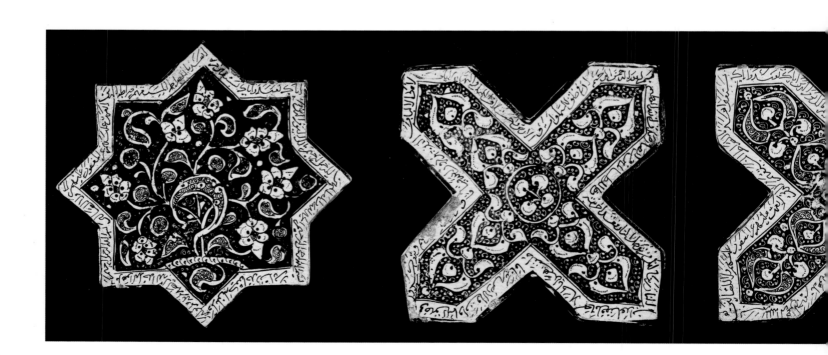

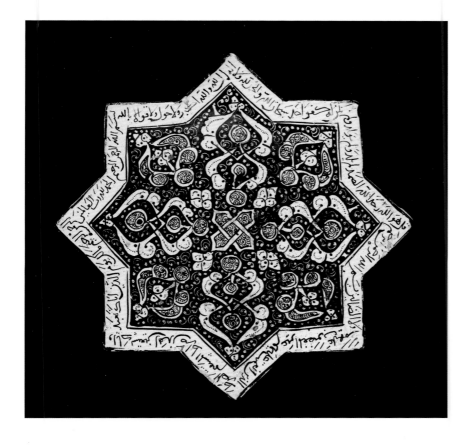

25.
A group of stone-paste star and cross lustre tiles, Kashan, central Iran, mid 13th century
31 cm (average diameter)
BM.1983.454; 478; 452; 451; 462, Godman Bequest; 1896,0210.1

These tiles are from a group of about 160 tiles that were once in the *Imamzade Yahya*, a shrine in the town of Veramin in Iran. Tiles, particularly those decorated in lustre were the main form of interior decoration of secular and religious buildings in medieval Iran at this time. They were made at Kashan, the principal ceramic production centre at this time.[1] The Arabic inscriptions around the edge of the tiles in *naskh* are from the Qur'an and one of the group is dated to the month of *Dhu'l Hijja* 660 H / August-September 1262 AD.

1. Porter 1995: 35; Watson 1985; Carboni and Masuya 1993: 15
VP

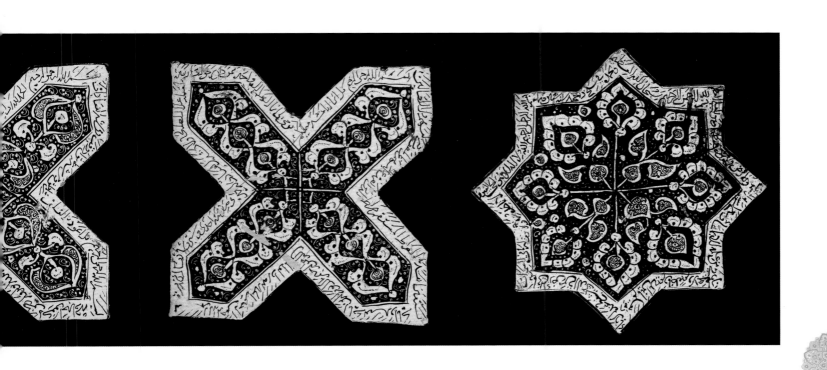

26.
**Eight-pointed stone-paste
star tile, cobalt and lustre
on a white ground, Iran,
Kashan, 13th – 14th
century**
20.5 cm (diam.)
BM.1878,1230.561

The main design on this tile [1] consists of a pair of seated figures, their figural features and tresses of hair typical of the Turkic invaders, the Seljuq Turks who came into the central Islamic heartlands in the 11th century. Around the edge of the tile in *naskh* is a verse of Persian poetry. '*Last night the moon came to your house, filled with envy I thought of chasing him away. Who is the moon to sit in the same place as you?*[2]' Love poetry is sometimes found on tiles in medieval Iranian shrines. The love they speak of is often the divine love of Sufi mystical poetry.

1. Hayward Gallery 1976: no. 385; Porter 1995:44
2. I am grateful to Abdullah Ghouchani for this translation. The poet is at present unidentified VP

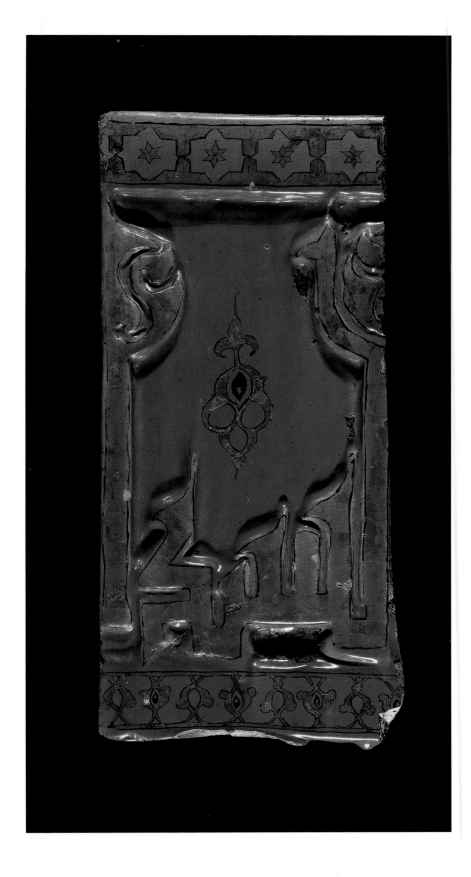

27.
Rectangular stone-paste tile, Kashan, central Iran, second half of the 13th century
35.2 cm x 16 cm
BM 1983.190 Godman Bequest

Against the turquoise blue ground with overglaze enamelled colours in red and gold, in a style known as *minai*, the angular letters stand out in relief. Although by the 13th century the angular *kufic* style had been largely superseded by the more legible cursive script *naskh*, the angular style was still used for monumental inscriptions. Here the tile with its single word is part of a frieze of tiles now dispersed [1]. They are likely to have been set into the wall of a shrine or a mosque.

1. Porter 1995: 41; Carboni and Masuya 1993: 10. The Metropolitan Museum of Art tile is from Qur'an 15:92. It is not clear what the word on this tile is. If the tile is part of the same frieze then one possibility is *ataynaka* which appears in verses 64 and 87 of the same *surah*.
VP

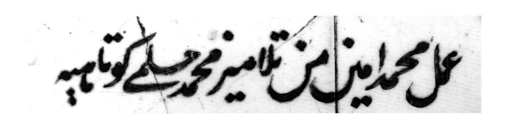

28.
Ottoman tile panel
Kutahya, Turkey
1315 H/1898 AD
130 cm x 93 cm
2003.7.1

The framed panel is made up of 6 x 4 attached underglazed tiles. The calligraphy displays the words: "Padeshah chogh yashar." Padeshah is the title of the ruler, and the phrase reads: "Long live the Padeshah."

The panel is dated to 1310 H/ 1893 AD and signed by Mohammed Amin the student of Mohammed Helmi of Kutahya. Kutahya is a famous city in Turkey, which was renowned for its underglazed tiles since the 16th century. The tradition of tile making survived up to the 19th/20th century when this panel was produced. It is most likely that Mohammed Amin the student of Helmi, supervised the application of his calligraphic

composition on tiles in Kutahya. Yet it is also possible that the Padeshah upon receiving this *lawha* or panel from the famed calligrapher, sent it to Kutahya to be duplicated on tiles.

The panel is a unique piece as it exemplifies the relationship between the master craftsman and his pupil in the Ottoman Empire. The signature shows that Mohammed Amin is the student of Mohammed Helmi. This manner of signature by which a student recalls his teacher is called the *silsilah* or chain. Mohammed (Mehmed) Helmi was a known calligrapher of the late 19th century. He supervised the *hilya* or the calligrapher's license of a young calligrapher

Mehmed Recai, who later referred to himself as Mehmed Racai, student of Abdurrahman & Helmi. Helmi also endorsed several *hilya* of renowned Ottoman calligraphers. The *silsilah* chain gives the calligrapher his status among other calligraphers and secures him fame and future commissions. The 19th century witnessed the culmination of a style of Ottoman tile work that had its origins at the ceramic centres of Iznik and Kutahya. This new style combined the technical expertise of Turkish tile making with the western decorative repertoire.
(Khalili collection, Vol. 5, p. 42)
HB

29.
Blue and white
Ottoman tiles
Ottoman Egypt or Syria
17th century
72 cm x 71.5 cm
2004.1.7

This tile panel consists of nine adjacent tiles in the form of a rectangle. The decorative composition consists of 3 round arches supported on long spiral columns. This architectural theme further depicts 3 finials on top of the arches, indicating that the arches are sections of domes. Hanging inside the arches are large glass oil lamps. The central arch is decorated with a cartouche inscribed with the phrase : "Upon God we depend". A bouquet of carnations and floral units spring out of a vase below the central cartouche. The flanking arches include the names Othman and Ali, while the names of the remaining righteous caliphs, Muhammad SAW and Allah are inscribed in the spandrels of the arches.

The blue and turquoise glazes' consistency changed and the pigment ran leaving a stained composition. The tile is of great interest due to the balanced dense composition, the beautifully inscribed calligraphy and the contrast between blue and turquoise on a white ground. The theme of the three arches is reminiscent of decorative units found in North Africa, while the appearance of zigzag and trefoil domes is a characteristic of the Mamluk dynasty. The carnation on the other hand indicates Ottoman patronage.
HB

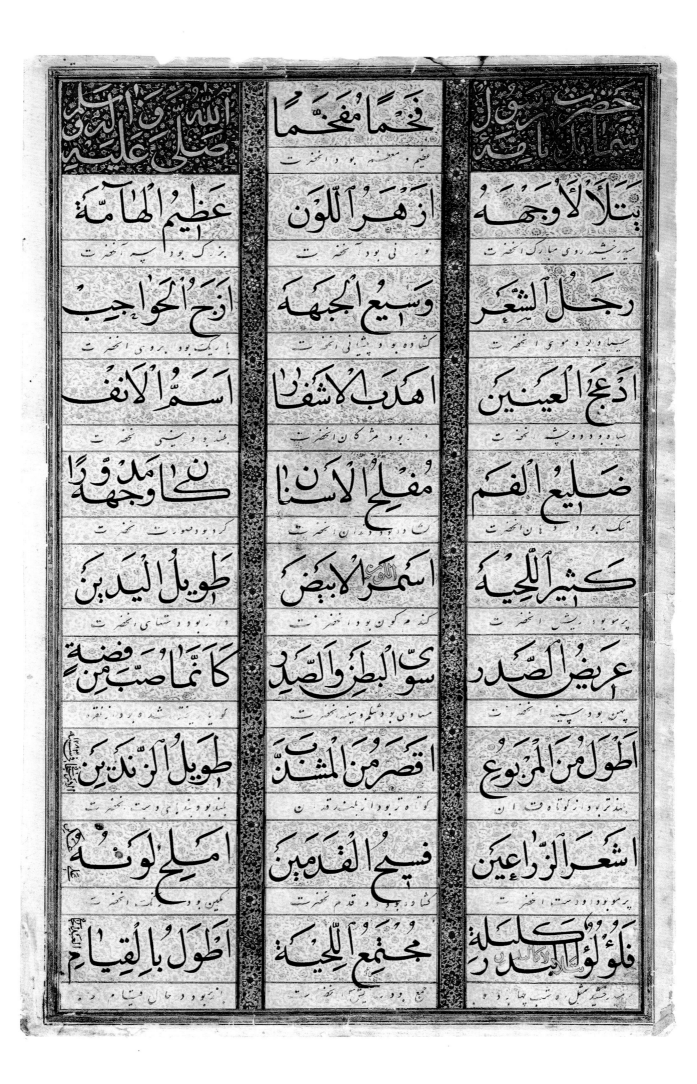

بسم الله — شمائل حضرت رسول

(ستون چپ)	(ستون میانه)	(ستون راست)
اللهُ وَاَرَاكَ صَلَّى اللهُ عَلَيْه	فَخْماً مُفَخَّماً	حضرت رسول شمائل یا نامه
عَظِيمَ الْهَامَة	اَزْهَرَ اللَّوْن	سَبْطاً لا وَجْهَه
اَزَجَّ الْحَوَاجِب	وَسِيعَ الْجَبْهَة	رَجِلَ الشَّعْر
اَشَمَّ الْاَنْف	اَهْدَبَ الْاَشْفَار	اَدْعَجَ الْعَيْنَيْن
مُدَوَّراً وَجْهَه	مُفَلَّجَ الْاَسْنَان	ضَلِيعَ الْفَم
طَوِيلَ الْيَدَيْن	اَسْمَرَ الْاَبْيَض	كَثِيرَ اللِّحْيَة
كَانَ مَا صَبٍّ مِنْ فِضَّة	سَوَاءَ الْبَطْن وَالصَّدْر	عَرِيضَ الصَّدْر
طَوِيلَ الزَّنْدَيْن	اَقْصَرَ مِنَ الْمُشَذَّب	اَطْوَل مِنَ الْمَرْبُوع
اَمْلَحَ لَوْنَه	فَسِيحَ الْقَدَمَيْن	اَشْعَرَ الذِّرَاعَيْن
اَطْوَل بِالْقِيَام	مُجْتَمِعَ اللِّحْيَة	فَلَوْلُؤٌ ...

30.
Illuminated large single folio *Shama'il Rasul Allah* – The physical description of the Prophet Muhammad SAW Iran , 1283 H/ 1866 AD
33.5 cm x 21.5 cm
2003.10.23

An illuminated single folio written in an elegant *naskh* script in Arabic with interlinear Persian translations. The folio is divided into three rows each containing 10 phrases describing the physical characteristics of the Prophet Muhammad SAW. The text is written in black ink on a richly decorated ground, filled with fine floral motifs in gold.

The folio is signed and dated by calligrapher Ali Askar Al Arsanjani in 1283 H./1866 AD, the son of calligrapher Muhammad Shafi'. Ali Askar continued the novelty of Al Nayrizi's *naskh* script and excelled in the *shikasteh* and *riqqa'* styles.
HB

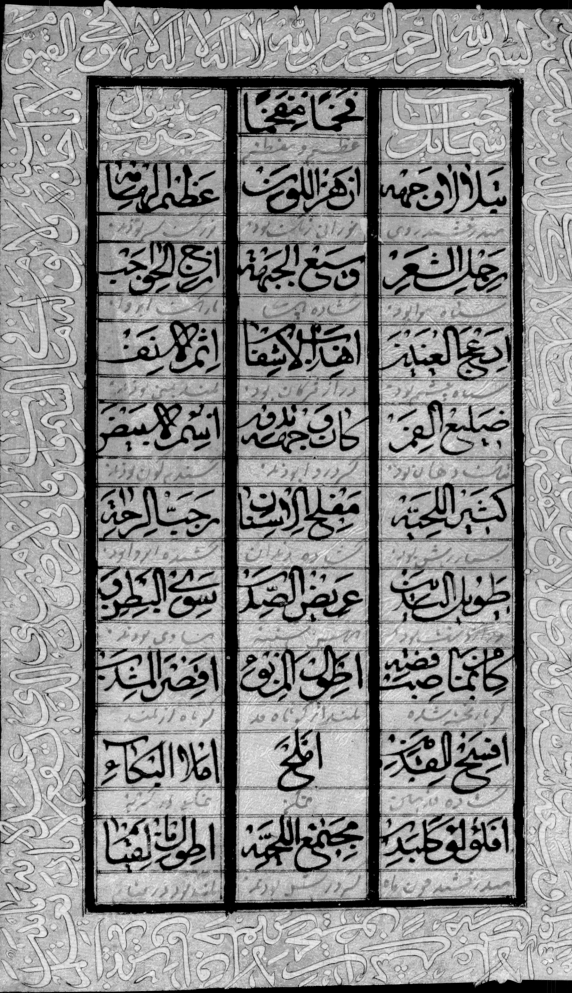

31.
Lacquered mirror & case
Qajar, Iran
c. 18th/19th century
15 cm x 23.5 cm
2001.1.182

The rectangular papier-mâché mirror case and cover are exquisitely decorated with polychrome intricate floral decorations on gold ground. The introduction of gold as a background dominated lacquered ware during the 18th century. The outer faces of the mirror reveal an intricate foliage decoration comprising a central oval shaped medallion, while the inner face of the mirror is decorated in calligraphy. The field directly opposite the mirror face contains attributes of the Prophet Muhammad SAW as recorded in the compilation titled "*Hilya Al Shami' I*". The attributes are recorded in three rows each of 10 lines with interlinear Farsi translations. The attributes are further framed with *Ayat Al Kursi* (the Throne Verse, *Surah Al Baqarah*: 225). The *hilya* or "adornment" is a calligraphic description of the physical appearance of the Prophet according to traditional Arabic accounts. Selections of the Prophet's physical description became a favoured theme in adorning wall hangings produced in Iran and Turkey, where it is believed that it would rejuvenate God's blessings.
HB

قَالَ الرِّضَا عَلَيْهِ السَّلَامُ الْأَصْحَابَهُ

عَلَيْكُمْ بِسِلَاحِ الْأَنْبِيَاءِ

قِيلَ وَمَا سِلَاحُ الْأَنْبِيَاءِ

قَالَ الدُّعَاءُ وَقَالَ الصَّادِقُ عَلَيْهِ

السَّلَامُ الدُّعَاءُ أَنْفَذُ مِنَ السِّنَانِ

الْحَمْدُ لِلَّهِ حَرَّرَهُ أَحْمَدُ النَّيْرِيزِي ١١٢٨

32.
Lacquered book binding
Isfahan, Iran
1128 H/1716 AD
23 cm x 14 cm
2003.6.27

The pair of papier-mâché book covers is divided into a decorative field and a frame that contains calligraphic cartouches. The field depicts a floral composition in yellow green and red against black background. The cover had been signed and dated by Ahmed Nayrizi son of Sultan Mohammed Shams Al-Din who was a master calligrapher and progenitor of the *naskh* style in 18th century Iran. He wrote prayer books, calligraphic exercises, and monumental inscriptions and also painted lacquer boxes. Towards the end of the 17th century, he worked under Shah Sultan Hussein in Isfahan, and signed his name as "Al Sultani", "that who is affiliated to the Sultan."

The inscription on the frame contains sayings of the Prophet Muhammad SAW that relate to the virtue of prayers. The first hadith reads: *"Shall I show you a weapon that will save you from your enemies and make your means of sustenance abundant? They say yes indeed. He said, Pray to your Lord night and day, for the believer's weapon is prayer."*

On the second leaf the hadith says: *"Depend on the prophetic weapon, they say, and what is this prophetic weapon? He said prayers. And the trusted one, peace be upon him added: Prayers are more effective than an iron spearhead."* Followed by the calligrapher's signature and date.

Lacquered surfaces appeared in the Islamic world towards the 15th century. They covered the surfaces of pen boxes, bookbinding and other papier-mâché based objects with varnished paintings. Historically they flourished in Iran, Ottoman Turkey, Central Asia and India. Numerous examples were produced in the court of the Timurid rulers in Herat, making the Herat school of lacquered items the model followed by other ateliers.
HB

"My God, I ask thee with your mercy which encompasses everything and with your sublime power that thee overtook with it everything..."

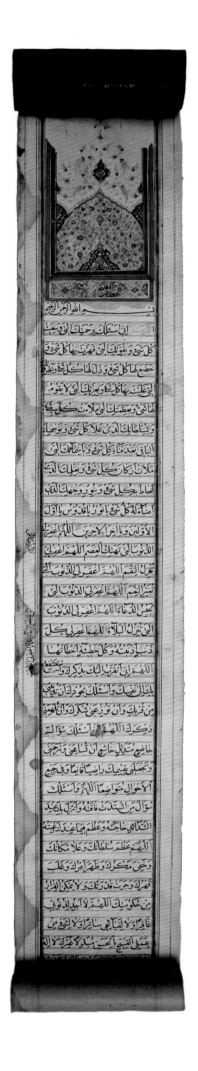

33.
A Prayer scroll on canvas
Isfahan, Iran
1247 H/1831 AD
Width 12 cm
2002.10.34

A long *doa'* (prayers) scroll written in Arabic was intended to be read on a Friday, according to the title panel. The title is beautifully illuminated in gold, red and blue. The script is written in simple *naskh* in black while the reference to God is made in red. Scrolls developed as an easy to handle and portable document used during the Friday speech or *"khutbah"*. This scroll was inscribed by Muhammad Hussein Ibn Muhammad Abu Al Qasim Al Isfahany in the year 1247 H /1831 AD. The canvas has witnessed minor repairs during its preparation.
HB

Beauty and Diversity

105

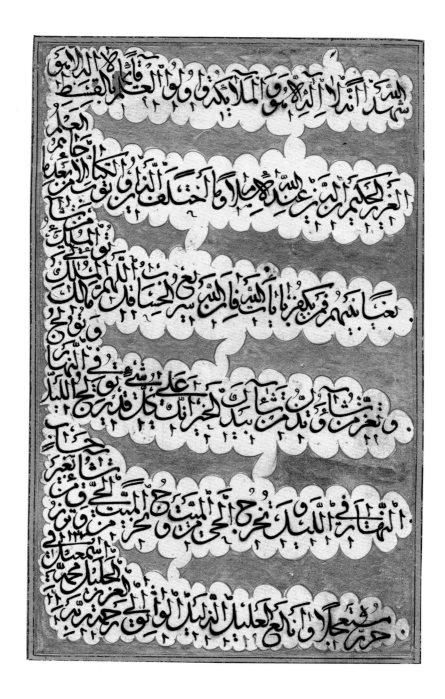

34.
Persian single folio
Surah Al Imran, verses 18,
19 & 26
Riqqa script inscribed by
Mohammed Ismail
1227 H/1812 AD
21.1 cm x 12.9 cm
1998.2.9

A single folio elegantly composed on white board with an orange border reveals the verses of *Surah Al Imran*: 18, 19 and 26. The calligraphy comprises of six lines of black text written within cloud shaped compartments outlined in orange against a gold coloured ground. The calligraphy reveals a highly structured composition, with rounded and densely structured letters. A dense agglomeration of letters is exhibited towards the extreme left side of the folio, leading the calligraphy to reach

upwards, almost touching the previous line. This style was adapted and favoured by the calligrapher Mohammed Ismail whose name is signed towards the end of the folio.

Mohammed Ismail was a renowned Iranian calligrapher and painter of lacquer ware. He is known to have favoured complex compositions. His work was charactarised by a strong western iconography. His brother Aqa Najaf was similarly a painter of lacquer work.

The *riqqa'* script is a cursive type of writing derived from the *thuluth* script. During the 19th and 20th centuries in Iran, it grew popular to revive the *reqqa'* (*riqqa'*) script and use it in copying verses from the Holy Qur'an.

A caskets signed by Mohammed Ismail, dating to 1288/1871 AD is found at the Historical Museum Berlin. (no. 71/23)
HB

35.
Part of a dark grey sandstone building foundation inscription from Bengal, eastern India, 885/1480.
43 cm x 40 cm
BM.1826,0708.2c
Presented by William Franklin

Bengal at this time was ruled by Shams Al-Din Yusuf Shah (1474-81) whose name is inscribed here. His capital was at Gaur where this inscription might have originated although it is unclear at the present time which monument it came from. In Bengal they perfected the script sometimes known as *tughra'i* which is an elegant variant of the *thuluth* script, the uprights of the letters creating a dense forest of columns through which words and letters are interspersed.[1] The whole inscription,[2] only a section of which is shown here (there are four other pieces from it) is dated to Sunday the 14th day of the month of *Muharram* year 885 (Monday 20 March 1480) and gives the sultan's titles and genealogy: '*the great and exalted sultan, Shams Al-Dunya wa'l Din Abu'l Muzaffar (father of the victorious) Yusuf Shah Al-Sultan Ibn Barbak Shah, Ibn Mahmud Shah, may God perpetuate his kingdom and sovereignty*'. The names of rulers in the Islamic world were often long and complex. In addition to stating the names of their father, grandfather and sometimes even further back, they included grand honorific titles known as *laqab*. Here our ruler is described as Shams Al-Dunya wa'l Din '*sun of the world and the religion*'.

1. Begley 1985
2. Sinha 2001: 134-43
VP

37.
**Silver seal of Gabriel
Harper inscribed in Arabic
script, 1199/1784-85.**
**7.2 cm (height), 6.4
(diam.)**
BM.1996,0325.1

36.
**Alabaster tombstone in
the name of Muhammad
SAW Sultan Baqir Al-
Ansari (died 405/1014-
15), probably Yazd, Iran
52 cm x 32 cm
BM.1982,0623.1**

Muslim graves are usually marked by upright stone slabs – one at the head, the other at the foot of the grave. There is a further example in the catalague. The epitaph has a dual function: to record the name of the deceased and to bear witness to his or her faith. [1] The text of the tombstone - which is inscribed in an elegant form of *kufic* where many of the ends of the letters have been turned into leaves - is divided into several sections. Around the margin starting in the bottom right hand corner is the *basmalah* ('In the name of God the Merciful the Compassionate') followed by the phrase, '*Thanks be to God, Lord of the Worlds and peace be upon Muhammad SAW and his family*'. In the centre is the name of the deceased, Sultan Baqir Al-Ansari and the date of his death 405/1014-15. [2]

1. Blair 1998: 196-199; Afshar 1976
2. At the top is the word Muhammad. It is not clear whether this is part of his name.
VP

Colonel Gabriel Harper was an important figure in the East India company and was based for some years in the state of Awadh in northern India which had been conquered by the British in 1764. He was appointed to the court of Shuja' Al-Dawlah (a puppet ruler of the British) in 1770 to command the troups based at Cawnpore. [1]The use of seals by East India company officials to validate documents followed a long tradition in Iran and India. Persian was the official language of the court in India until the mid 19th century and the British used it for many purposes including for their seals. In elegant *nasta'liq* script against a floral background the seal is inscribed :

'*Sir Afraz Al-Dawla (exalted of the state) Bahadur, Colonel Gabriel Harper Asad Jang (lion of war) servant of Shah 'Alam Padshah Ghazi (victorious king) and the regnal year 27*'. This last refers to the Mughal emperor Shah Alam II (1760-1806)

1. Porter 1997: 27
VP

38e.

38g.

38j.

Islamic Coins

Coins are not only an essential adjunct to the study of Islamic history but, as inscribed and dateable objects, they are a key element in the study of the uses of writing and calligraphy in Islam and the chronological and regional developments of the Arabic script. The coins and glass stamps grouped here offer a snapshot into different script styles, languages and types of inscriptions from the beginnings of Islamic coinage in the 7th century to coins of the later dynasties of Iran and Turkey. [1]

1. For some general books on the subject: Broome 1985; Mitchener 1977; Album 1998.

Beauty and Diversity

109

38a.
Coin weight in the name of Ubayd Allah Ibn Al-Habhab,
Finance Director of Egypt between 725 and 734.
3.5 cm (diam.), 6.47 g
BM. OA 4162

Weights made of glass were produced in Egypt from the 8th century. They were struck by the department of weights and measures for a variety of purposes. They often contain the phrase *waf* meaning full weight, as the primary task of the Finance director was to ensure that no cheating took place in the market-place. The two examples included here were made in the Umayyad period (661-750), the first of the Muslim dynasties that, with their capital at Damascus ruled the Islamic empire at this time.

The legends on this weight[1] are introduced by the words 'in the name of God' followed by Ubayd Allah's name who 'ordered a weight of a *fals* of four and thirty *qirat* full weight'. The term *qirat* is a synonym of *kharruba*, or carob seed, which had been used as a unit of weight since before the Islamic period, and derives from the Greek *keration*. It was the denomination of the earliest *fals*, the term used to describe a copper coin. The legends on the weight are in a simple angular *kufic* script.

1. Morton 1985: no. 42

38b.
Ring weight in the name of Al-Qasim Ibn Ubayd Allah, Finance Director of Egypt between 734 and 742, dated 118/736-37
3.8 cm (diam., irreg.), 149.4 g
BM.OA 4354

This cloudy green weight, [1] damaged on one side, was made to weigh meat. It is inscribed in the same angular *kufic* script as on the disk weight: 'in the name of God, the Amir Al-Qasim Ibn Ubayd Allah ordered in the year eighteen and hundred, honesty for God, a *ratl* of meat, full-weight'. The weight of the *ratl* in the Umayyad period was roughly 440 gm. (approximately one pound, this example is lighter because it is fragmentary). It has been suggested that its shape in the form of a ring and with a large hole through the middle enabled these weights to be suspended together by a cord.

1. Morton 1985: no. 91

38d.
Arab-Sasanian silver dirham struck at Isfahan, 60/679-80.
3.2 cm (diam.), 4.05 g
BM.1935,0303.11
Presented by C. Davies Sherborn

This was struck by Ubaidallah Ibn Ziyad, who was appointed governor of Khurasan in north-eastern Iran by the Caliph Mu'awiya in 672 AD. He then became governor of Basra and Kufa in Mesopotamia in 679 AD.

The coin [1] shows on the obverse the portrait of the Sasanian king Khusrow II (ruled 591-628) wearing a winged crown, the symbol of the Zoroastrian god of victory, Verathragna. The coins legends are in Pahlavi/Middle Persian and follow the

38c.
Arab-Byzantine copper *fals*, struck with the mint name Iliya, (the Latin name for Jerusalem) Filastin, the province of Palestine.
2.1 cm (diam.), 3.55 g
BM.1933,0213.8

This *fals* [1] was struck at Jerusalem during the reign of the Umayyad caliph Abd Al-Malik (685-705) one of the major figures in Islamic history and builder of the Dome of the Rock in Jerusalem. This coin shows clearly on one side (the obverse) the influence of Byzantine coins: the cursive 'm' which was a denomination (40 *nummi*) of the late Byzantine monetary system. This is combined with the mint name, Iliya Filastin, in Arabic in *kufic* style but using a combination of the Latin name for the city and the Arabic name for the province. The reverse of the coin shows a figure who is described as 'a standing Caliph', presumably Abd Al-Malik himself, bearded, with a sword, and around him the religious formula 'Muhammad SAW is the Prophet of God'.

1. Lane Poole 1875: no. 82

Sasanian tradition: name of governor on the right and GDH *apzud* (may his glory increase) on the left. Sasanian astral symbols and the Arabic *basmala* appear in the margin. The reverse depicts a Zoroastrian fire altar and two attendants. Again, the legends are in Pahlavi and astral signs are shown in the margin. The mint is abbreviated to letters GD on the left (Gay Isfahan, central Iran).

1. Walker 1941: 100 (c4)

38e.
**Umayyad gold *dinar*,
struck in 128/745-746
18.5 cm (diam.), 4.27 g
BM.1870,0709.5**

This coin [1] inscribed in *kufic* script, was struck after the main monetary reform which took place in the late 690s, during the reign of Abd Al-Malik, as part of the 'Arabisation' of his empire. Although it bears no mint name it is likely to have been struck in Damascus. This reform consisted mainly of introducing a standard weight of 4.27 gm to the gold coinage, and religious legends instead of the figural imagery that had been used on coins hitherto. The obverse is inscribed with most of Qur'an chapter 112, whose words state the very essence of Islam, 'God is alone, God is eternal, He begets not nor is He begotten'. Around the margin is the date, year 128 of the Hijra calendar, introduced by the formula 'In the name of God, this *dinar* was struck'. The central inscription of the reverse is part of the *shahadah*, the Islamic profession of faith: 'There is no God but God, He is alone and has no partner', while the marginal inscription focuses upon the prophetic mission: 'Muhammad SAW is the Prophet of God sent with guidance and the religion of truth to make it prevail over all other religions although idolaters may be averse to it'. (Qur'an 9: 33).

1. Lane Poole 1875: No. 40

38f.
**Abbasid silver *dirham*,
struck at Madinat Al-Salam
('The city of peace',
Baghdad) in 181/797-98
2.6 cm (diam.), 2.53 g
BM.1979,0404.13**

Struck during the reign of the Caliph Harun Al-Rashid (786-809), the obverse shows the *shahadah* and in the margin the mint and date formula. On the reverse, the marginal legend is Qur'an 9: 33 (as on the *dinar* described above). The central field is inscribed 'Muhammad SAW is the Prophet of God'. Below it is the phrase: 'the Amir Al-Amin Muhammad son of the Commander of the Faithful ordered [this coin] and Ja'far'. Al-Amin was the caliph's heir but his succession was contested by his brother Al-Ma'mun. This resulted in a bloody civil war in which Al-Amin was defeated. Ja'far is Ja'far Al-Barmaki, his tutor and father's powerful vizier.

38h.
**Abbasid gold double *dinar*,
struck in Baghdad, first
half of 13th century
2.7 cm (diam.), 3.67 g
BM.1884,0703.32**

This was struck by of one of the last Abbasid caliphs, Al-Mustansir (1226-42) before the Mongol conquest and the destruction of Baghdad and the Abbasid caliphate in 1258. It is inscribed with the traditional religious formulas in an embellished and elegant *kufic* script. [1]

1. Lane-Poole 1889: No. 503 a

38g.
**Fatimid gold *dinar* struck
at Tripoli (North Africa),
447/1055-56
2.1 cm (diam.), 4.09 g
BM.1849,1121.120**

The Fatimids, who ruled North Africa before Egypt and Syria (969-1171) adopted legends written in concentric circles for their coins. The Fatimids were Shi'a and the *kufic*-style religious legends clearly demonstrate their Shi'i affiliations with the phrase, 'Ali is the Favourite (or friend) of God'. Another phrase states: 'the *imam* summons all men to profess the unity of the eternal God'.[1]

1.Lane-Poole 1879: No. 152

38i.
**Hafsid gold *dinar*, struck in
North Africa, mid 13th
century.
2.8 cm (diam.), 4.72 g
BM.1886,0503.1**

This was struck by Abu Abd Allah Muhammad 1249-1277), the second ruler of the Hafsid dynasty whose domain comprised present day Tunisia and eastern Algeria (1228-1574). The Hafsid gold coins are characterised by the use of an elegant form of *maghribi kufic*, the script which developed and was adopted in the 10th century in Spain and North Africa. This coin is a double *dinar*, the primary denomination of the gold coinage during the 13th and the 14th century. It bears neither mint nor date, only the religious formulae 'thanks be to God' and 'there is no power or strength except in God' and the full name of the ruler as 'Commander of the Faithful'.

1.Lane-Poole 1890: No. 160k

38j.
Ayyubid dinar, struck in Cairo, 631/1233-34
2.1 cm (diam.), 7.06 g
BM.1856,0916.3

In Egypt and Syria, during the reign of the Ayyubid sultan Al-Kamil (1218-38) the cursive script *naskh* replaced *kufic* on all the denominations of the currency. This change took place nearly a century after the cursive script had begun to be introduced on monumental public inscriptions under an earlier ruler of Syria, Nur Al-Din Zangi (1146-74). [1] The *dinar* [2] is inscribed with the Sultan's name, 'Al-Malik Al-Kamil Abu-l-Ma'ali Muhammad SAW Ibn Abi Bakr' on one side, and the name of the Abbasid caliph Al-Mustansir on the other. As God's representative on earth, all rulers pledged spiritual allegiance to the caliph publicly on the coinage and elsewhere until the overthrow of the caliphate by the Mongols in 1258.

1.Tabbaa 1994: 129
2.Lane Poole 1879: No. 395

38k.
Mamluk gold *dinar*, struck in Cairo by Al-Ashraf Nasir Al-Din Sha'ban, 779/ 1377-78
2.65 cm (diam.), 3.48 g
BM.1884,0608.12

The inscription is set within a lobed cartouche and consists of the names and titles of the sultan on one side and the *shahadah* on the other in a fine script resembling *thuluth*, the script favoured by the Mamluks.

1.Lane-Poole 1889: No. 607e

38l.
Anonymous gold *dinar*, struck in Sijilmassa, 13th century
2.9 cm (diam.), 4.55 g
BM.1879,1002.43

This coin is an example of a new style of coinage introduced in North Africa and Spain by the Almohad dynasty (1147-1269). It was struck at Sijilmasa in present-day Morocco, a key town in medieval times because of its strategic position on the gold route to West Africa. The central square is the dominant feature of the design and the *kufic* script has been replaced by the cursive *naskh*. All the legends are religious in content. The obverse has the phrase 'God the One and Only, Muhammad SAW is the Prophet of God, the Qur'an is the word of God'. and below, the mint name, Sijilmassa. In the margin 'In the name of God, the Merciful, the Compassionate,

38m.
Silver *dirham* of the Seljuqs of Anatolia, struck in Konya, 640/1242-43
2.2 cm (diam.), 2.91 g
BM.Marsden 89

These rulers of Anatolia were Turks but were strongly influenced by Persian culture. They spoke Persian at court and on their coinage they adopted imagery such as the lion and sun motif from the pre-Islamic Iranian past. They also favoured ancient Persian names which feature in the ancient myths and legends of Ancient Iran. In this case it is Kaykhusraw II, son of Kaykubad (1236-45). [1] As could be seen with the Ayyubid *dinar* above, the rulers pledged spiritual allegiance to the Abbasid caliphs in Baghdad. In this case it is the Caliph Al-Mustansir (1226-42). The style of the script is an exuberant cursive, ornamented with dots, florets and stars.

1.Lane-Poole 1877: No. 216

God bless our Lord Muhammad SAW, there is no God but God, He is the Merciful, the Compassionate'. The reverse is inscribed with the phrase 'Praise to God and favour to God and power and might to God'. The marginal inscription reads 'He is the One and the Last, the Apparent and the Secret, and He is Omniscient of everything'. There is neither date nor the name of the sovereign on this coin, but it may be dated to the late Almohad dynasty or to the early Marinids (1196-1465).

1.Lane Poole 1880: No. 215

38n.
Silver *dirham* of the Seljuqs of Anatolia, struck in Siwas, 646/1248-49
2.2 cm (diam.), 2.74 g
1852,1023.19

This *dirham*, [1] struck by Qilij Arslan IV (1248-57), is directly inspired by a previous Mongol issue of the Great Khan Ulush Beg (642-43/1244-45) featuring a mounted archer. Since their victory in 1243, the Mongols were the nominal overlords of the Seljuqs and they paid the Mongols an annual tribute. The legends are in *naskh*, ornamented with dots and florets. On the obverse is the ruler's name: 'The very great Sultan Izz Al-Dunya wa'l-Din Qilij Arslan son of Kaykhusraw Companion of the Commander of the Faithful'; on the reverse, the Caliph's name, Al-Musta'sim (1242-58), the last of the Abbasid caliphs in Baghdad. Figural coins are relatively rare in Islam and this is one of the few moments when it was clearly acceptable to use such imagery.

1.Lane-Poole 1877: No. 247

39o.

39r.

39t.

A Group of Mongol Coins

The Mongols were in origin Shamanist peoples of the Central Asian steppes who came to rule vast swathes of Central Asia, China and the Near-East from the 13th century. They were descendants of the Mongol Genghis Khan (1206-27) and a branch of them, the Ilkhanid dynasty established themselves in Baghdad in 1258, overthrowing the last of the Abbasid caliphs there. Ilkhanid silver coins are interesting for a number of reasons: their high degree of purity; the range of innovative designs introduced on them, the legends they bear, sometimes in the languages reflecting their Mongol origins, *Uighur* or *'Phagspa* (aTibetan language) and the use of different styles of script. [1]

1. Blair 1983, AK Akce 1992

39o.
Ilkhanid double *dirham*,
struck by Ghazan Mahmud
at Jazira, 699/1299-1300
2.5 cm (diam.), 4.26 g
BM.1922,0717.71

While the *shahadah* is inscribed on the obverse in Arabic *kufic* script, testifying to the Mongols' recent conversion to Islam, the reverse highlights their Far Eastern origins. The inscription which includes the name of Ghazan Mahmud (1295-1304) appears in three scripts: his name, Ghazan Mahmud, in Arabic (*naskh*) and '*Phagspa* , and the phrase 'By God's power Ghazan's coinage' in *Uighur*.

39p.
Ilkhanid six *dirham* coin,
struck by Uljaytu,
Nishapur, Iran, 1304-17
3.5 cm (diam.), 12.85 g
BM.1981,1108.3

Uljaytu (1304-17) went through phases of adherence to various religions: Shamanism, Christianity, Buddhism. Once he had accepted Islam he then oscillated between Sunnism and Shi'ism committing himself to Shi'a Islam in 1308. This is reflected on his coins. On the obverse, the Islamic Profession of Faith is inscribed in an ornamented *kufic* with the addition of the Shi'a phrase 'Ali is the friend of God'. Around the margin are the names of the twelve Shi'a *imams* in cursive script which is also used on the reverse for the ruler's name and titles.

39q.
Ilkhanid silver *dirham*,
struck by Abu Said, Siwas,
Anatolia, 734/1333-34
2 cm (diam.), 2.85 g
1972,0814.34

This coin combines a number of interesting features both in terms of its calligraphic styles and the use of different alphabets. Associated with their Mongol origins in Central Asia is the script *Uighur* which on this coin is used to inscribe the ruler Abu Said's name, while his titles are in Arabic in *naskh* script. Also emphasizing their Mongol roots is the use of the Ilkhanid era year 734 (1333-34). On the reverse in the margin are the names of the Orthodox caliphs in *naskh* while in the field the *shahadah* is inscribed in a remarkable manner – the *kufic* script is rendered extremely angular and written in the form of a square. This style of writing thought by some to be derived from Chinese seal script, was used to great effect on architecture during the Ilkhanid era and subsequently on all other objects such as gravestones and seals. All Abu Said's coins struck in the years 733-34/1332-34 bear this design.

39r.
Safavid double *dirham,*
struck by Shah Abbas II,
Tabriz, 1069/1658-59
3.6 cm (diam.), 9.15g
BM.1865,0804.41

During the reign of Abbas II (1642-67) different scripts and languages were used for different purposes. While the *shahadah* on the obverse is in Arabic and in *naskh*, on the reverse are Persian couplets glorifying the ruler written in *nasta'liq* script: 'Throughout the world imperial coinage came, struck by God's Grace in Abbas the second's name'. [1]This contrasting use of *naskh* for religious inscriptions in Arabic and *nasta'liq* for poetry is typical of inscriptions on the other arts of the Safavids such as metalwork.

1.Lane Poole 1887: No. 39

39s.
Safavid twenty *shahi* silver coin struck by Shah Sultan Husayn, Isfahan, 1109/1697-98
5.2 cm (diam.), 37.12 g
BM.1920,0616.2

The predominant script here is a fine example of *nasta'liq* particularly popular for the writing of inscriptions in Iran from about the 16th century. Of additional interest here is the prominent placing on the obverse of the coin – along with the *shahadah* – of the names of the twelve *imams* revered in Shi'a Islam. These were inscribed on a coin of the Ilkhanid ruler Uljaytu but their appearance on coins had been intermittent since then. During the reign of Sultan Husayn (1105-35/1694-1722), Shi'ism became more prominent in Iran with less tolerance shown to Sunnis and other minorities. The appearance of the *imams* on the coinage is therefore highly significant as a public affirmation of the growing influence of the Shi'i clerics at this time.

39t.
Ottoman gold coin, one *onluk*, struck by Ahmad III, at Constantinople in 1115/1703
2.6 cm (diam.), 3.48 g
BM.1877,0703.17

The *tughra* was the intricate device that served as the imperial monograms of the Ottoman sultans of Turkey. First adopted on documents and coins from the 14th century, it does not appear regularly on the coinage until the reign of Ahmed III (1703-30). Each sultan generally chose the precise form of his *tughra* on the day of his accession from specimens prepared for him in advance.[1] Ahmed III's *tughra* on this coin,[2] which is embellished with arabesques and florets is inscribed, 'Ahmad son of Mahmud Khan the Victorious (Al-Muzaffar) the ever victorious'.

1. Nadir 1986: 14
2. Lane Poole 1883: No. 436

39u.
Ottoman gold coin, a *zeri mahbub* or double sequin, struck by the Ottoman sultan Mahmud I, 1143/1730
2.4 cm (diam.), 4.33 g
BM.Marsden 464

On the obverse is the Sultans' *tughra*.[1] On the reverse is the mint name Islambul (Istanbul), which in Turkish means 'Where Islam abounds', and was given to the city following its conquest under Mehmed II in 1453 as an alternative for Constantinople. It is first used as a mint name during the reign of Ahmad III and a *firman* of 1760 decreed that it should be substituted for the mint name Qustantiniyya on coins but it continued to alternate with it until 1807. Unlike other Islamic coinages, the Ottoman sultans did not place religious phrases on their coins.

1. Lane Poole 1883: No.507

Arabic Script as Pattern

Interest in the Arabic script as a decorative pattern developed in different parts of the world. In the newly Islamic regions, the Arabic letters were perceived as a sacred pattern that was associated with the language of the Quran. Yet when the script reached non-Muslim regions, the script became merely a remarkable decorative pattern.

The Arabic script reached Europe via trade, during the 13th century. Mamluk metal work, woven and embroidered material, carpets, ceramics and glass were imports that found way into treasuries of private collections in Europe. The textile patterns included *tiraz* bands with Arabic inscriptions, reminiscent to the coronation gown of Emperor Frederick II (13th century). The 'Veneto-Saracenic' metal vessels from the Mamluk period, were made with a blank space in the shape of shields so the European customers could commission the addition of their heraldic emblem. On ceramics the Hispano-Moresque School excelled in producing Lustre jars in the spirit of the famed Alhambra vase, which continued to be produced in Spain and Italy with pseudo inscription bands.

The greatest interest in the script as pattern and the perception of the letters as mysterious signs flourished during the Orientalist period. In 1489 Breydenbach of Germany published the first appearance of the Arabic script in a printed book. The decorative script inspired Renaissance artists and in many paintings pseudo Arabic adorned valuable art objects.

When Islam was introduced to regions such as Africa, Central Asia, Persia, Southeast Asia and China the Arabic script was difficult and different from the native's script, where few people could read and write. In the earliest stage where the citizens were not familiar with the Arabic language, the script became a pseudo- decorative element included in art objects as commitment of their adherence to Islam, and as an appeal for God's blessings.

The objects considered so far have included a range of written texts in a variety of script styles but whose primary purpose however decorative the inscription has been to communicate. In the following group, the primary purpose is to decorate and thus we see designs based on Arabic letters. In the case of the Iznik bowl, there are illegible phrases while on the other pieces, groups of letters have been turned into attractive patterns.

40.
Large footed bowl, Iznik,
Turkey, c. 1510-20
23.5 cm (height), 42.5 cm
(diam.)
1897.0618.1

The sheer size of this bowl makes it a technical tour de force and, with its elaborate decoration, it was clearly a prestige object. [1] It has been suggested that bowls such as this were used by people of rank for their ritual ablutions before prayers either in mosques or in private; cleanliness before prayers being encumbent on all Muslims. The Arabic inscription on the outside of the bowl is an integral feature of the design and yet what is interesting is that it appears to be meaningless. The letters are in *naskh*, making up what seem to be a phrase repeated twice. Further study has not so far repaid its decipherment although it is perhaps based on a religious inscription or a verse of poetry. As with the mosque lamp, the inclusion of undecipherable inscriptions sometimes alongside perfectly legible ones, is a recurrent feature of Iznik objects in the early blue and white phase (ca 1490s – 1520s). [2] One can speculate about whether this was deliberate or designed by potters who knew no Arabic.

The intricate blue and white designs are strongly influenced by the decoration on Chinese blue and white porcelain that was imported into Turkey at this time, and of which the Turkish sultans had a large collection that can still be seen at their palace, Topkapi Saray, in Istanbul today [3]. Iznik was the main pottery production centre for Ottoman Turkey and made fine stone-paste wares for the court and other patrons from about the 1490s to 1700.

1. Atasoy & Raby 1989 no. 299
2. Atasoy & Raby 1989 nos. 60, 87, 105-8;
3. Krahl 1986
VP

118

41.
Stone-paste *albarello* with fluted sides painted in olive lustre against a cobalt blue ground, Damascus, Syria, 14th century.
36.2 cm (height)
BM.1983.266 Godman Bequest

Containers such as these, [1] painted in lustre and other techniques, were used to export luxury items from the Middle East to Europe such as oils, ungents and spices. These Damascus jars were well known in Europe and frequently listed in the records of medieval apothecaries. The Arabic which is in a loose *thuluth* script is a repetition of what are probably benedictory phrases but so stylised that their meaning is lost and the words turned into pattern.

1. Godman 1901: plate VI; Lane 1957: 15-17
VP

42.
Hemispherical brass bowl with lid inlaid with silver, gold and an organic black material, Syria, late 15th century
14.0 cm (diam.)
BM. 1878,1230.698

This belongs to a group of wares that were made for the European market – possibly in Damascus, which was known for its inlaid brass work in the Mamluk period and which was frequently visited by Venetian merchants.[1] They are often designated by the term 'Veneto-Saracenic' because they were originally believed to be the work of immigrant craftsmen from the Islamic world working in Venice. This theory has now been disproved but nonetheless these metal objects were to have a great impact on northern Italian metal production of the 15th –16th centuries. The designs on this vessel include European coats of arms and pseudo-inscriptions which are based on so-called 'plaited' *kufic* a style popular some three centuries earlier. The intention was to give an impression of writing only. It is this kind of 'pseudo-writing' that is picked up by some of the Renaissance artists.[2]

1. Ward 1993:115; Ward et Al. 1995: 235-258
2. Contadini and Burnett 1999; Ferber 1975
VP

43.
Lustre painted tin-glaze Hispano-Moresque jar, Andalucia (southern Spain) c. 14th-15th centuries.
36.5 cm (height)
BM. 1983.542 Godman Bequest

This vessel [1] was made in the domain of the Nasrid sultans (1232-1492) whose capital was at Granada. The techniques of tin-glaze and lustre are among the great contributions of the Islamic world to the West. Both techniques were developed in 9th century Iraq, spread to Egypt and probably from there to Spain. By 1300 the first centre at Malaga was well established. The well known Moroccan traveller Ibn Battuta who visited Malaga in 1350 described how 'wonderful golden pottery' was made in the city and that it was 'sent abroad to far distant lands'. [2] The techniques were later transferred to Italy and had a strong impact on Italian majolica. On this vessel, the 'Arabic script' in cobalt blue is rendered purely as pattern and consists of a series of letters *alif lam ayn alif* (possibly an abbreviation of '*Al-afiya*' meaning 'good health') contained within panels repeated along the bottom and the side.

1. Godman 1901: No 458.
2. Caiger-Smith 1985: 86; Frothingham 1951

VP

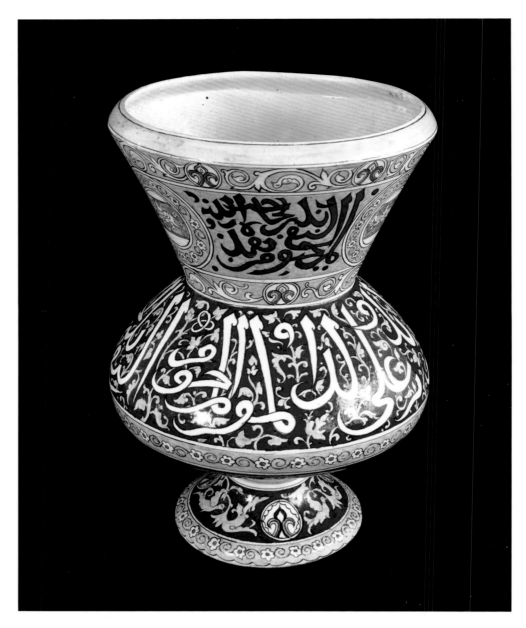

44.
Mamluk-inspired ceramic
mosque lamp
Italy
19th -20th century AD
34 cm x 22 cm
1998.2.267

Inspired by Mamluk mosque lamps produced in Egypt and Syria during the 15th century, this outstanding ceramic mosque lamp reflects a period where Europeans were inspired by the fable of the Orient. The bulbous body of the Mamluk inspired mosque lamp is decorated with a band of pseudo calligraphy of Arabic letters, in white against blue. Originally the lamp would have incorporated the opening lines of *Surah Al Nur* (24:35): *"God is the light of the earth and heavens"*.

The neck of the lamp displays a second band of inscription intersected by roundels which host blazons or emblems of the royal patron. The background vegetal decoration imitates the continuous arabesque stems and leaves developed during the Islamic eras.

The function of Arabic calligraphy changed from delivering a message to serving as a decorative pattern, during the 18th and 19th century in Europe. Its contents and meanings became undecipherable, yet it was the pattern that characterised the mirage of the Muslim Orient.
HB

45.
A Theodore Deck "Persian blue" basin
Sevre, France
19th century
11.5 cm x 23 cm
2001.1.98

An outstanding ceramic basin, recalling the shape of medieval Mamluk metal basins, successfully captures the beautiful epigraphic cartouches and the oriental figurines within roundels. The back of the basin is decorated in a highly organised continuous palmette shaped pattern, creating a multisided star with a central star medallion. The entire basin is glazed in lapis lazuli blue. The decorations which emboss the surface appear in lighter blue while the sunken ground attains a very dark blue tone. The interplay between the two shades of blue has attributed to making a masterpiece of the artwork.

The master calligrapher must have had an actual model in front of him to produce with such accuracy the letters and words on the basin. Reminiscent to the Mamluk metal basins, the name and dedication to the sultan in a monumental *thuluth* script, occupy the cartouches adorning the body of the basin. The letters appear in the foreground with spiral arabesques in the background. The fact that several of the same basins were produced at the same atelier indicates the preparation of a carefully planned pattern that had guided the ceramist.

Théodore Deck (Gebweiler 1823-1891 AD) Sèvres was one of the pioneers of French ceramists during the late 19th early 20th century. He was the father of numerous techniques in the world of ceramics, such as lustre painting and "Persian blue". He was the author of "La Faience", a book revealing all the secrets of ceramics. His fame culminates when he became the director of The Manufacture Nationale at Sèvres.

He was the mentor for several trained disciples, who continued producing and exhibiting in Paris and Europe. HB

46.
Calligraphic frit ware dish
Maastricht, Holland
20th century AD
5 cm x 26 cm
1998.1.3995

Pottery production flourished in Maastricht, Holland in the late 19th early 20th centuries. Oriental designs and Arabic calligraphy were perceived as part of the allure of the mysteries of the orient. The dish displays eight names written in cursive style in black against a white background. The names are that of the four righteous caliphs: Abu Bakr, Omar, Othman and Ali, alternating with four names of angels: Mikhail, Gabriel, Israfil, and 'Azrail. At the centre of the dish, in a circular composition the words: Muhammad SAW the Prophet, hand of Rahman. The plate was presumably inscribed by Rahman, as the calligraphy reflects a hand that is well versed in Arabic calligraphy.

The presence of the names of the four righteous caliphs was a popular decorative element in Ottoman Turkey and the appearance of the names of the angels and archangel had developed as a popular addition recognized by other religions. Angels were numerously mentioned in the Qur'an and Hadith, they are portrayed as noble messengers of God, obeying his orders and delivering his messages. (81:20-21).
HB

47.
Lustre polychrome Alhambra style vases
Seville, Spain
13th century H/19th century AD
Height 35.5 cm
2003.6.42
2004.4

The Arab traveller and historian Ibn-Batutta recorded in his accounts on Spain: "At this place, the beautiful gilded pottery and porcelain which is exported to the most distant countries is manufactured." During fourteenth century, the productions of lustrous vases on a large scale were known as the Alhambra vases. Alhambra vases stood high over four feet tall, inspiring Spanish and Italian factories up to the 18th and 19th century. Several workshops emerged in Europe engaged in pottery work and producing oriental fritware objects; the island of Majorca, Seville and Malaga. Today the spirit of the Alhambra vase survives and continues to inspire and capture the admiration of viewers.

The Alhambra vase attains a special shape, with its egg shaped body, flaring top and two winged handles at its side which spring vertically. The decoration incorporates geometric patterns, floral scrolls and at their centre is a belt of stylized Arabic letters. The overall effect is termed hispano-moresque, a style that reverberated the mysteries of the Orient.

The pseudo-inscription band combines the earliest *kufic* style with their rigid vertical characters with the later cursive *naskh* style, revealing its free flowing curves. The non-arab designer masterly created a design that has shed an Oriental vivacity on the vase.

Alhambra vase became a popular decorative unit for Orientalist artists. Rudolf Ernst (1854-1932) included two examples of the vase in his oil painting La Terrasse.[1] In an exquisite scene on an oriental veranda, the Alhambra vases are placed on the sides of the stair case. They were illustrated with a great degree of precision known to Ernst. The central calligraphic band in lustre against a buff ground and their blue winged handles outlined in red gives the impression that the artist must have been acquainted with such vases.

1. Thornton, 1994, p.156
Christie's London, auction catalogue June 2001, p.72.
HB

Islam
in China and the Malay World

Because it is incumbent upon Muslims to learn the Qur'an in its original Arabic, Arabic spread with Islam, and the Arabic language was often learnt alongside local languages; the Arabic script often displaced local scripts. Arabic has therefore been employed to write a whole variety of languages such as Persian (Iran), Urdu (India), Dari (Afghanistan), Ottoman Turkish (until the reforms of Ataturk in 1928, when it was displaced by the Roman alphabet), and, until recently, the languages of Indonesia and Malaysia. Wherever there were Muslim communities, however far afield, we find the Arabic script.

Muslims first came to China as traders in the 8th century in the age of two great empires: in China the T'ang dynasty (618-906), in the Islamic world, the Abbasids (750-1258) with their capital at Baghdad in Iraq. Up to about the 10th century, Arab ships were sailing all the way to China stopping at the Indian Ocean ports and S. E. Asia along the way. The intrepid sailors and merchants such as the fabled Sinbad would set off on journeys that lasted years and return with exotic goods, one of the most popular items of which was porcelain, which was in great demand in the Near-East at this time. As a result of the trade, Muslims settled along the South China coast; at Quanzhou are the gravestones of hundreds of Muslims who came as merchants from as far afield as Iran and Yemen.

During the Ming dynasty (1368-1643), in particular in the late 15th to early 16th century, there was a powerful Muslim minority at the court of Beijing. Its importance can be seen by the many mosques built by them at this time, and in the numbers of blue and white porcelains and bronzes inscribed in Arabic script. The earliest known examples of these bear the reign marks of Emperor Hongzhi (1488-1505) (Cat. no. 60) while the bulk seem to date from the following reign of Zhengde (1506-21). These inscriptions are generally poetic, benedictory, or Qur'anic in nature and written in a characteristically fluid style which is typical of Chinese-Arabic. This style of inscription appears in other contexts, such as Qur'ans and gravestones. Sometimes legible, at others it is clear that the artist knew no Arabic and was simply copying words he had seen (Cat.no. 63). This characteristic Chinese-Arabic calligraphic style is evident even in the 19th century scroll where the calligraphy has an abstract beauty representing a unique synthesis of Islamic and Chinese aesthetics (Cat. no. 65).

The importance of the Malay world and China must be highlighted. The Malay world; Sumatra, Aceh and the Malay Peninsula, emerged as important trade centers. They were the links between the West and China. This section emphasises the contributions these regions had on the development and continuation of the art of Islamic calligraphy (Cat. no. 54).

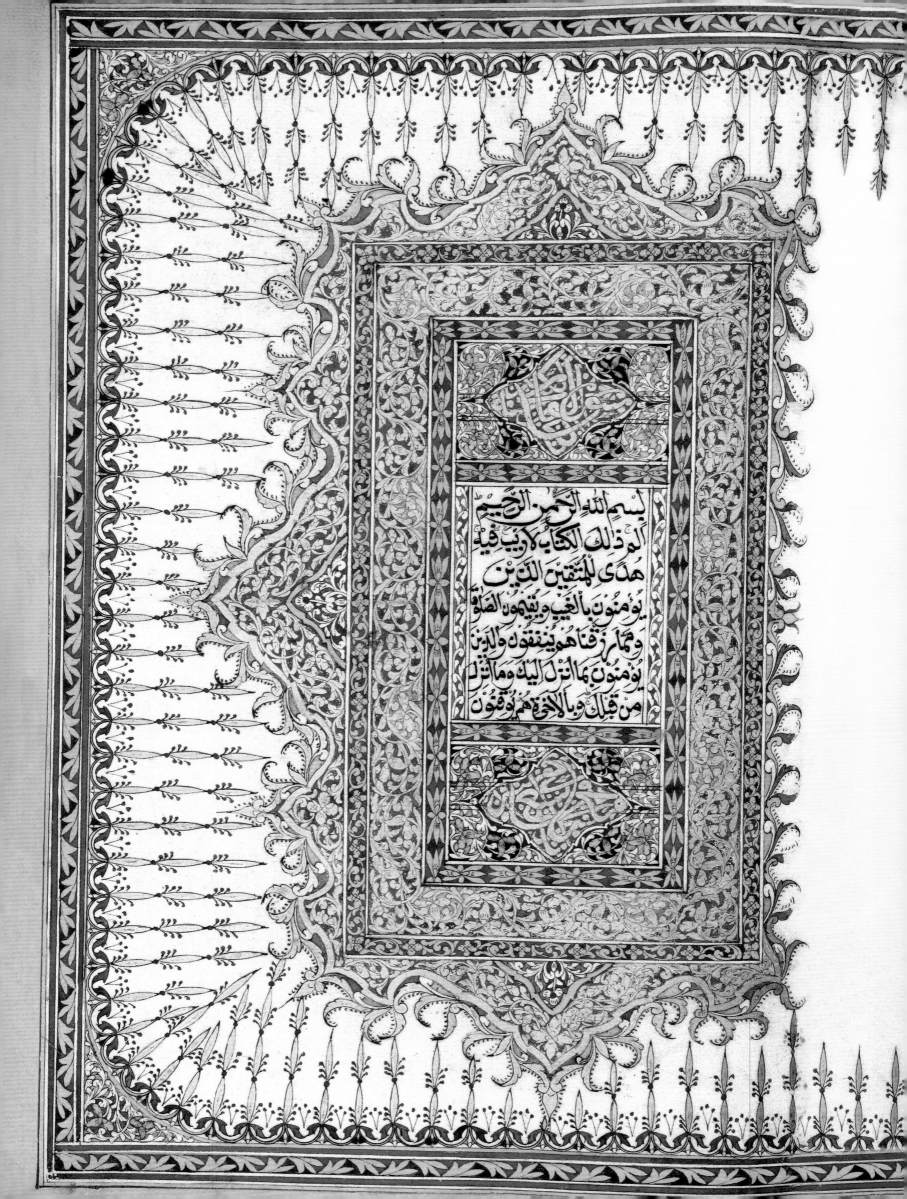

بِسْمِ اللَّهِ الرَّحْمَنِ الرَّحِيمِ
الم ذَلِكَ الْكِتَابُ لَا رَيْبَ فِيهِ
هُدًى لِلْمُتَّقِينَ الَّذِينَ
يُؤْمِنُونَ بِالْغَيْبِ وَيُقِيمُونَ الصَّلَاةَ
وَمِمَّا رَزَقْنَاهُمْ يُنْفِقُونَ وَالَّذِينَ
يُؤْمِنُونَ بِمَا أُنْزِلَ إِلَيْكَ وَمَا أُنْزِلَ
مِنْ قَبْلِكَ وَبِالْآخِرَةِ هُمْ يُوقِنُونَ

48.
Complete Malay Qur'an
Terengganu, The Malay Peninsula
19th century AD
43 cm x 28 cm
1998.1.3427

Known as "the Gold Edition", this complete Qur'an is an example of royal patronage in the north west of the Malay Peninsula. It is believed to have been copied for the Sultan of Terengganu, Sultan Zainal Abidin II, (1793-1808) who also founded the Abidin Masjid in Terengganu. The Gold Edition displays outstanding illuminations on its frontispieces and end pages. The decoration represents distinct Malay features such as tessellation coming inwards from the page borders into the text section, vegetal leaves and scrolls in harmony with the surrounding environment and framing the beautiful *naskh* script, as well as quadripartite leaves known as *bunga tanjung* motifs. All the apparent motifs reflect the long tradition of woodcarvings and batik printing in Terengganu. The overall composition is similar to the woodcarvings of the entrance gateway at Pusara Tok Pelam, Kuala Terengganu.

Gold was a colour reserved and featured in manuscripts of royal patronage. Red, blue and black pigments added to the overall outstanding composition of the illuminated frontispieces. The ink used for calligraphy is called Iron gall ink, which in time attacks the pages, producing a charred effect of calligraphy on paper.

Good quality Iron gall ink was easily prepared, as the ingredients were inexpensive and readily available. It was stable when exposed to light, with perfect consistency and suitable for reed pens and brushes; accordingly it became popular among calligraphers. Yet Iron gall ink slowly revealed its self-destructing properties known to conservators as Iron gall ink corrosion, destroying the manuscript pages.

Few pages after the last *surah* of the Qur'an, a text box indicating the articulation marks was added for further reference. The box which is dated to 1288 H/1872 AD may have been added at a later period.
HB

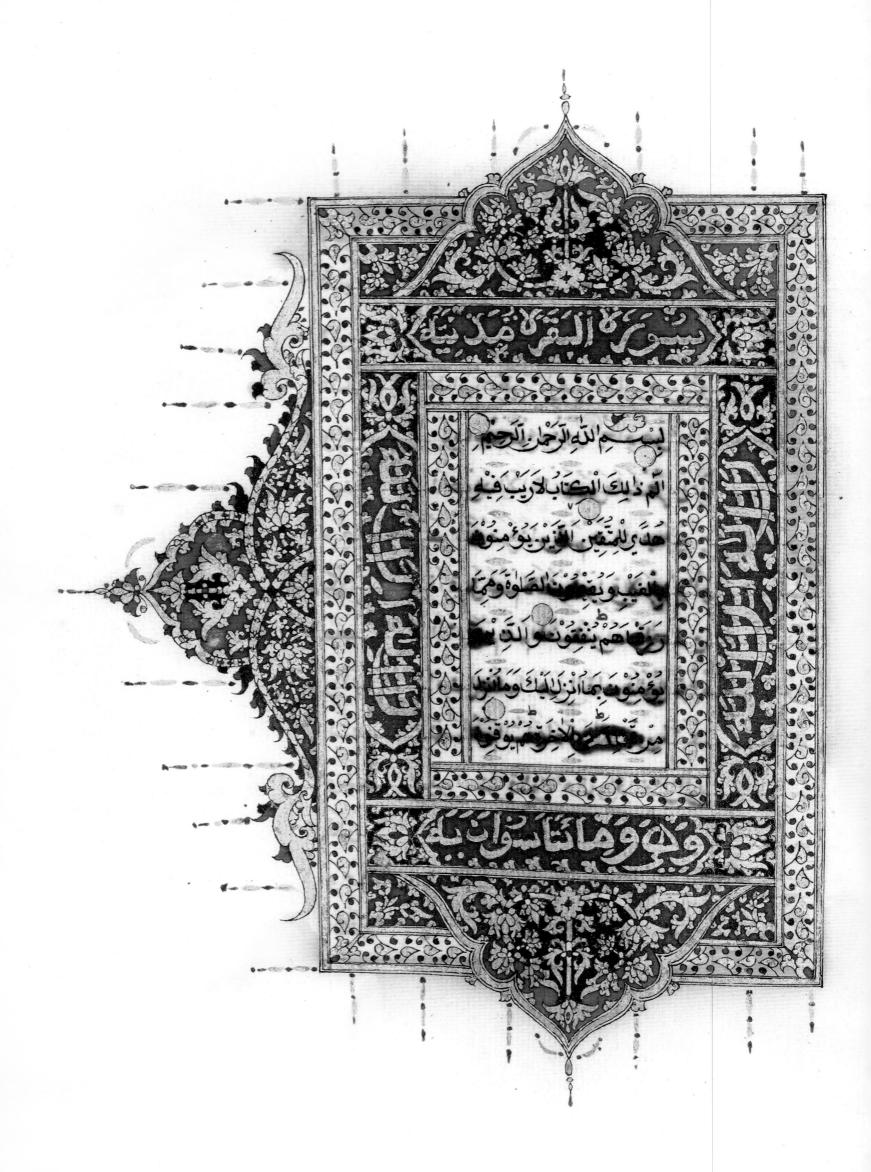

بِسْمِ اللَّهِ الرَّحْمَٰنِ الرَّحِيمِ

الم ذَٰلِكَ الْكِتَابُ لَا رَيْبَ فِيهِ

هُدًى لِّلْمُتَّقِينَ الَّذِينَ يُؤْمِنُونَ

بِالْغَيْبِ وَيُقِيمُونَ الصَّلَاةَ وَمِمَّا

رَزَقْنَاهُمْ يُنفِقُونَ ۝ وَالَّذِينَ

يُؤْمِنُونَ بِمَا أُنزِلَ إِلَيْكَ وَمَا أُنزِلَ

مِن قَبْلِكَ وَبِالْآخِرَةِ هُمْ يُوقِنُونَ

سُورَةُ الْبَقَرَةِ مَدَنِيَّةٌ

وَهِيَ مِائَتَانِ وَسِتُّ ...

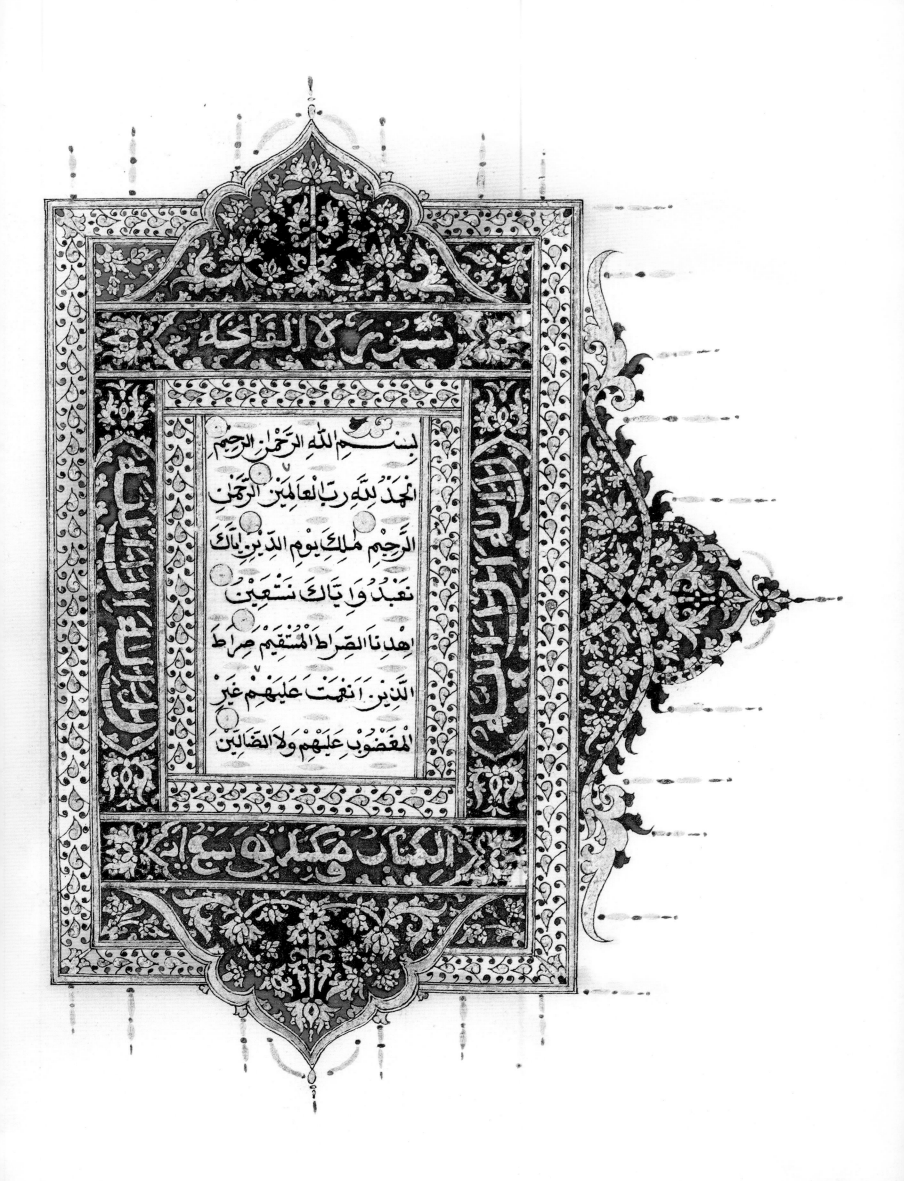

سورة الفاتحة

بِسْمِ اللّٰهِ الرَّحْمٰنِ الرَّحِيْمِ
الْحَمْدُ لِلّٰهِ رَبِّ الْعَالَمِيْنَ الرَّحْمٰنِ
الرَّحِيْمِ مَالِكِ يَوْمِ الدِّيْنِ إِيَّاكَ
نَعْبُدُ وَإِيَّاكَ نَسْتَعِيْنُ
اهْدِنَا الصِّرَاطَ الْمُسْتَقِيْمَ صِرَاطَ
الَّذِيْنَ أَنْعَمْتَ عَلَيْهِمْ غَيْرِ
الْمَغْضُوْبِ عَلَيْهِمْ وَلَا الضَّالِّيْنَ

الكتاب مكتبة نور النبع انه

49.
A single volume Qur'an
Terengganu, Malay
Penisnsula
19th century
22 cm x 18 cm x 5 cm
1998.1.3500

An example of a Southeast Asian unsigned Qur'an copied in the 19th century in Terengganu, Malaysia. It is written in *naskh* with a peculiar manner of articulation reminiscent to the prevalent Jawi script. *Surah* headings are emphasised, and divisions of the text to *juz'* (chapters) are indicated in the margin.

The frontispieces are decorated in vegetal scrollwork that is paralleled to the wood carving traditions of the region. In an unorthodox manner, a new identity sprang out of the individual cultures of Southeast Asia to express and share in the heritage of the Qur'an illumination.

To the Malay world, wood and woodcarving harmoniously reflect their close connection to nature and their environment. Malay-Muslim art relied heavily on incorporating nature in their decorative repertoire and reflecting the inner symbolism beyond these motifs. The Malay Qur'an similar to the local woodcarvings displays leaves and spirals filled with the *Bunga tanjung* motifs: continuos winged leaf scroll, and the *bunga teratai* : Lotus flower, as well as the *Gunungan:* mountains vegetal composition at the sides of the written text.

The lightly polished cream paper is European in origin with watermarks dating the manuscript to the early 19th century.
HB

50.
Qing dynasty Qur'an
China
17th century AD
27 cm x 19.5 cm
1998.3.50

The complete 30 *juz'* Qur'an from the Qing Dynasty displays a unique style of Arabic calligraphy which developed in China. This style, known as Sini Arabic, moulds the Arabic alphabet in a way so as to adhere to patterns, creating images and filling empty units. Each *juz'* of the Qur'an is bound in a dark varnished leather binding decorated in gold with lotus blossoms and cloud scroll foliage. The traditional Chinese decorative motifs frame a calligraphic roundel; a verse from the Qur'an: *"None shall touch but those who are clean"* (56:79).

Each *juz'* displays several illuminated pages, where green, blue and red decorations form the border of the pages. Each folio is divided into text box and decorative contour. The page displays three lines of calligraphy, each hosting a few words. The border decoration is an expression identifying with both Islamic and Chinese concepts. Arabic script was incorporated within designs such as half moons and flags, inspired from the Chinese culture and heritage. The border decorations extend into the margin from the ornamental frame, in a manner popular to Chinese Qur'ans produced during the Qing dynasty. For the Chinese calligrapher, writing the Arabic language represented a religious duty for which God would grant him merits and blessings. The Chinese calligrapher used different strokes to create the shape of the letters: with curves, formal, perpendicular, spiral and oblique strokes, the Arabic letters became a form of art. The dots common to many letters of the Arabic scripts were rendered as nail-heads, used in different locations to add to the flow of the composition.
HB

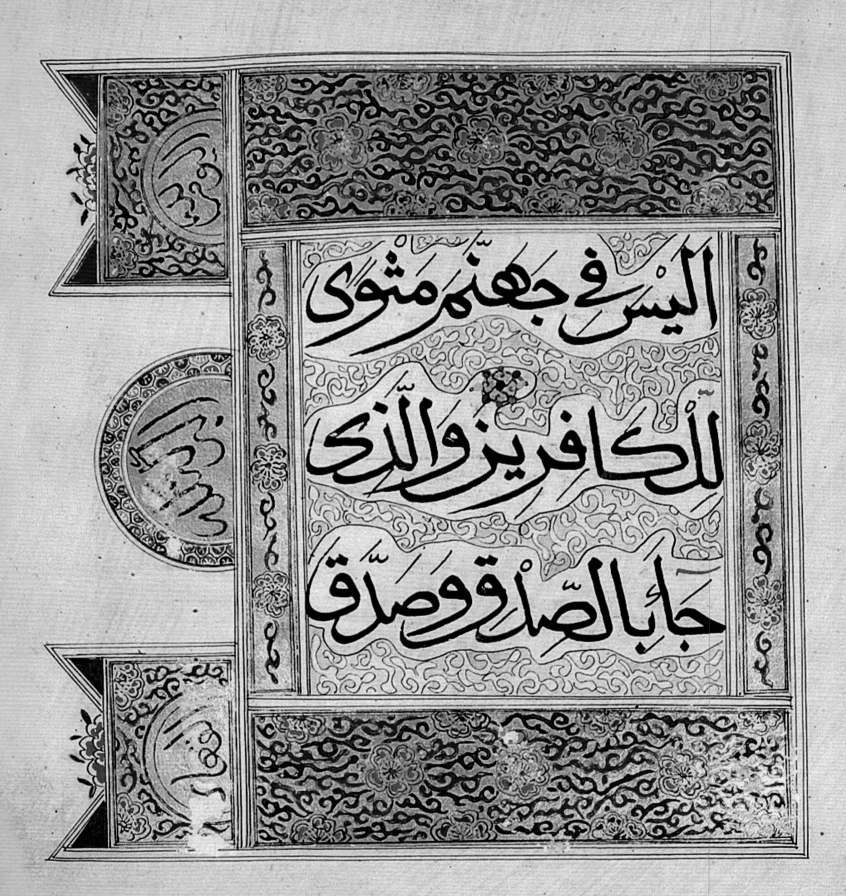

اليس في جهنم مثوى

للكافرين والذي

جاء بالصدق وصدّق

فَمَنْ أَظْلَمُ مِمَّنْ كَذَبَ عَلَى اللَّهِ وَكَذَّبَ بِالصِّدْقِ إِذْ جَاءَهُ

اِهْدِنَا الصِّرَاطَ
الْمُسْتَقِيمَ صِرَاطَ
الَّذِينَ أَنْعَمْتَ
عَلَيْهِمْ غَيْرِ
الْمَغْضُوبِ عَلَيْهِمْ
وَلَا الضَّآلِّينَ

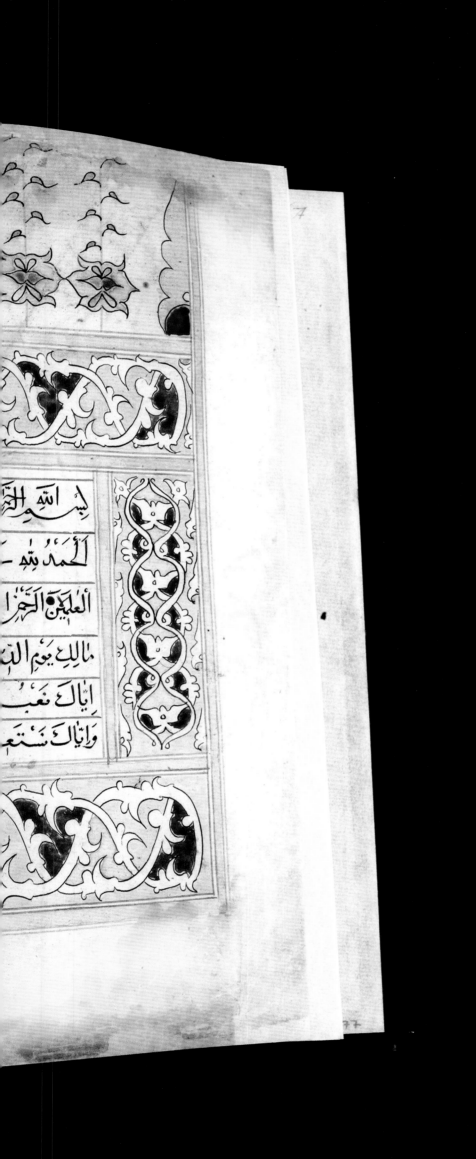

51.
Illuminated Qur'an transcibed by Ali Dibr Ibn Abd Al Karim Al Kanjuky
Mindanao, Pilippines
1299 H/1881 AD
35 cm x 22 cm
2001.1.177

This large illuminated Mindanao Qur'an signed and dated, becomes a unique addition to the Islamic realm of Southeast Asia. The manuscript consists of 469 folios, with 12 lines per page copied in bold *naskh* script. The colophon gives the name of the calligrapher as Ali Dibr Ibn Abd Al Karim Al Kanjuky, at the Archipelago in the city of Mindanao.

The decorated frontispiece exhibits a design of continuous floral scrolls surrounding the text box and creating a *surah* heading. Islam came to the Philippines around the 13th century and gradually spread in the southern region especially in the areas represented today by Tawi-Tawi, Sulu, Basilan, Maguindanao, Cotabato and Lanao. In the early 15th century, Sharif Muhammad Kabungsuan, an Arab-Malay preacher from the royal house of Malacca, settled down with a local princess, and founded a sultanate whose capital was Cotabato. The Malay influence in the floral designs and colour scheme is visible throughout the manuscript.
HB

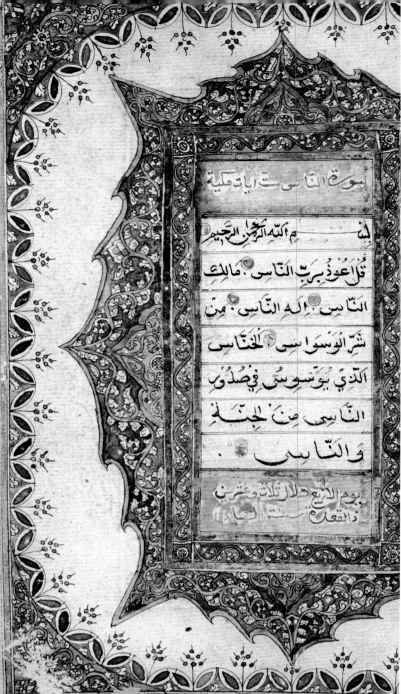

52.
Hand written Quran
Java, The Malay World
1261 H/1845 AD
30 cm x 20 cm
2004.2.2

The handwritten Quran begins with a prayer and a short remark in Javanese which indicates the date to be 1248 H/1832 AD. The frontispiece contains a text box, which is in multiple frames. The characteristic of the frames is their intertwined waves that lead out to the three side arches. The corners of the page create a beautiful addition to the decorative text box and its surrounding. They give the folio its boundary and reveal the use of small crenellated like designs similar to those found in manuscripts from the East Coast style. Red, bright blue and golden yellow appears as the desirable colour combination. The end frames are similarly decorated with outer brackets yet the text box is more centered and its frame emerges from its four sides. The calligraphy used is

53.
Hand written Quran
Java, The Malay World
19th century AD
30 cm x 20 cm
2004.2.3

This beautiful illuminated Quran from the Malay world makes use of blue, red, gold and black to enhance the decorative frontispieces. The text box is wide and the surah headings are in red. The framing decorations consist of flower and leaf branches, while the page brackets are filled with continuously growing scrolls against the white background. The black corner decorations found in the end frame shows a strong resemblance with the rattan weaving, a popular traditional craft in Southeast Asia. The paper watermark shows a lion within a roundel with a crown on top, indicating a 19th century production.
HB

simple *naskh*, with diacritic marks in a lighter colour and the verse divisions in gold. This manuscript also reveals the centerpiece in a very different decorative vocabulary, perhaps a later addition, or as is common to East Coast style, a combination of different features.

The paper possesses a watermark, three crescents, a shield with a crescent inside and the letters V & G. This type of paper is known to have been the product of the atelier of Andrea Galvani. The watermark confirms the date of the manuscript to the first half of the 19th century.
HB

54.
Goatskin parchment
The Malay Archipelago
18th –19th century
62 cm x 57 cm
1998.1.5694

The parchment has two *Surahs* of the Qur'an written within its text box. The text box is placed within a monumental frame decorated with scrolling floral and geometric motifs in red, black, gold and green. Similar to the Qur'an folios the parchment hosts marginal medallions, on each side, containing letters in gold against red, green and black ground. The crown of the folio , includes calligraphic inscriptions of which only the first word indicating a *doa'* or prayer can be deciphered. The first *surah* recalls *Surah Al Alaq*, or *Iqra'*, (96) while the following *Surah Alma'un* is (107). These two *Surahs* do not follow each other in the Qur'an, hence their presentation in this sequence is inexplicable.

The upper right corner contains a 16 square alphabet grid. Letter grids were popular as talismanic units, providing the owner with protection and good fortune. The inscribed letters are: Sa, Lam, Mim, Ha.

Parchments of goatskin were not available in abundance within the Malay world. Parchments needed cleaning, stretching and treatment before being available as writing ground. The decorative pattern used within the parchment suggests local patterns with an influence from India or the Middle East.
HB

55.
Cotton cover
The Malay World
1357 H/19th century
220 cm x 140 cm
1998.1.4096

This large cotton cover was produced in the Malay world presumably to commemorate the annual pilgrimage; the Hajj. The textile is filled with calligraphy from all directions. Its center is divided into rows, the first of which displays 13 long minarets, three domes, one of which is of greenish colour. This row contains the date and few words indicating that this is a depiction of Mecca and Medina (the two holiest cities of Islam). The Prophet's burial chamber is indeed roofed by a green dome. The second row includes the sentence: *"this is what the merciful has promised",* above images of the Holy Kaaba, Mecca.

Surrounding the entire decorative part of the cover is *Ayat Al Kursi*, written in modern *naskh* script, followed by the names of the four righteous caliphs. The cotton cover also displays the *Shahadah* and in a medallion the phrase: *"Allah is the ever lasting."* In spirit, the cover is reminiscent to the black Kiswa cover that drapes the Holy Kaaba. It was perhaps hung in the houses or doors of those who have recently performed this spiritual journey.
HB

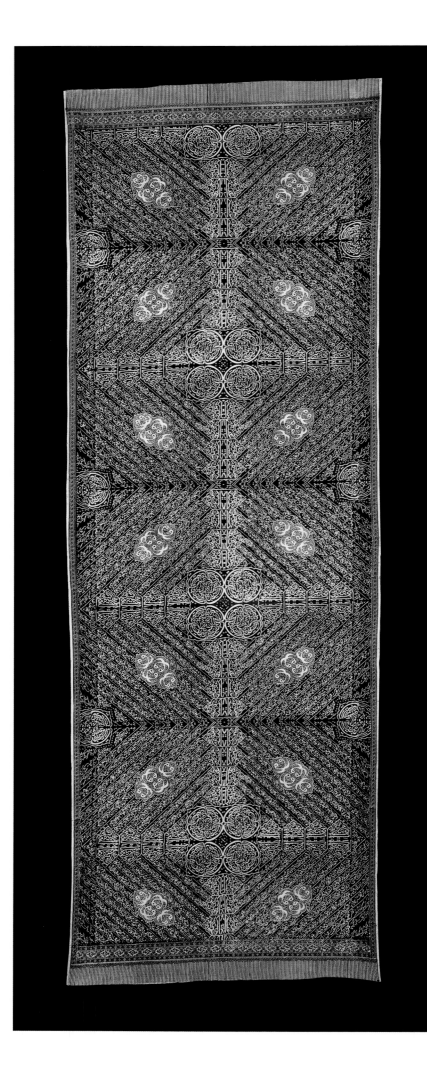

56.
Cotton textile, blue and white batik, Java, Indonesia, early 20th century
266 cm x 89 cm
1993,0412.01

While there had been contacts between Indonesia and the Islamic world through trade since early medieval times, Islam was only adopted in Indonesia in the 15th century and rapidly became the dominant religion. Trade and pilgrimage were undoubtedly factors influencing the designs of cloths such as this remarkable batik. [1] There were imported Indian cloths and carpets circulating in the region and the pilgrims to Mecca are certain to have seen the magnificent covering of the Ka'aba (the *kiswa*) and other calligraphic textiles. The function of cloths such as these is unclear. One suggestion is that they might have been worn as protection by warriors (*pendekar*) going into battle. The inscriptions which are in mirror image on the textile, consist of the names of the Prophets that appear in the Qur'an, after each of which is the formula, *'Peace be upon him'*.

1.Kerlogue 2001
VP

57.
Enamelled belt buckle
The Malay Peninsula
20th century
18.5 cm x 10 cm
1998.1.4277

Placed at the center of a leather or cloth belt, this enamelled belt buckle is both functional and its decorative calligraphy renders it as talismanic. The oval shaped unit is decorated with a central lozenge which contains a 3 x 3 grid. The grid combines letters and numbers, the key letters are Ya, Lam & Ta, and F. These letters combined creates the Arabic word *Ya Latif*; *'you who are kind',* a phrase which calls upon Allah with one of his 99 names. The lozenge is further placed within a bed of floral scrolls a decorative motif popular in the Malay world. HB

58.
Chinese bronze container with bamboo design on the rim and base and lion-head handles, six-character Xuande mark, 1426-35
11 cm (height)
BM. 1883,1020.6

In two cartouches on either side of the vessel are clumsily written versions of the *shahadah*, inscribed in the fluid style typical of Arabic written in China. This is one of many surviving bronze objects with Arabic inscriptions made for Chinese/Muslim patrons. [1]

1. Laufer 1934
VP

59.
Chinese porcelain incense burner, Ming dynasty
Zhengde mark, 1506-21
12.5 cm (height)
BM.1973,0726.367

Porcelain censers such as these [1] would have been used by members of the Chinese elite at temples, mosques or at home for burning incense sticks, powders or pellets made from vanilla, aloes, wood or camphor – its scent released after heating on charcoal. The Arabic inscriptions in the roundels translate as follows: *'I am the tender-hearted, ask for me, you will find me, pray for me do not seek any other than me'*

1. Harrison-Hall 2001:198
VP

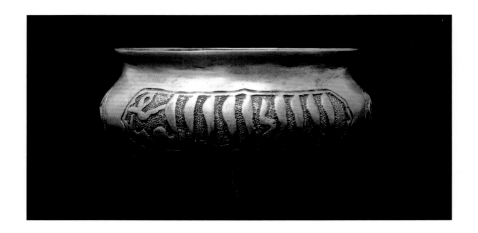

60.
Cast bronze incense burner
Ming dynasty, China
Early 15th century
8 cm x 14 cm

Incense burners appear in the Chinese market as early as the 15th century. In cast bronze or enamelled cloisonné, they bear the *Shahadah* (the profession of faith). This cast bronze incense burner has around its globular body three calligraphic cartouches, which bear the two parts of the *Shahadah*, and a thank God gratitude message ("*Afdal*" meaning the best). Burning incense was a tradition taken from the Prophet who burned insence on Fridays. The burner has a stamp on its base of the Ming dynasty's reign of Xuande (1426-35 AD). The stamp is in Chinese characters as it was stamped by officials during this period. The simplicity by which the calligraphy creates a repeated rhythm, gives this burner its charm and harmony.
HB

61.
Cast bronze vase
China,
17th-18th century
18.7 cm x 11 cm
2000.2.119

A long necked bronze vase with a bulbous body and two round ring handles is a shape commonly utilized in ceramics produced in China. The bronze vase is decorated with two calligraphic medallions. Each inscribed in cursive Arabic, phrases of thanks and gratitude to God. Such vases survived in abundance due to their durable material. They were presumably used as decorative units at home and exported to the Muslim markets.
HB

"Subhan Allah"

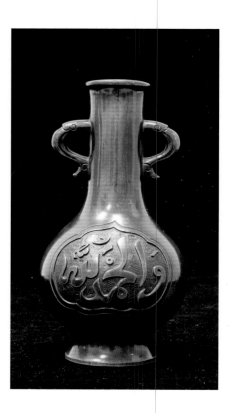

152

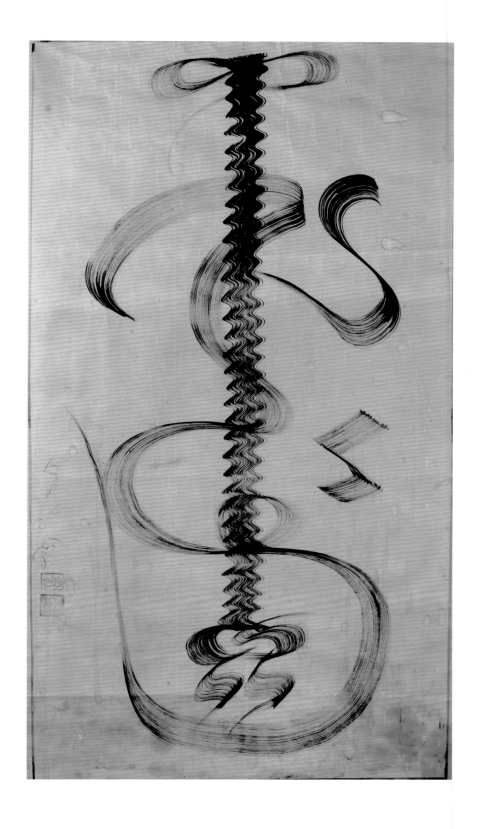

62.
Arabic calligraphy, black ink on paper, probably southern China, c. 19th century
125 cm x 76 cm
BM. 2002,0729.01

This remarkable calligraphy is an extraordinary blend of Chinese and Islamic aesthetics, produced with a brush – in the rest of the Islamic world, calligraphy is written with a pen. The word *ya* (oh) is written vertically with *Rahim* (Compassionate), horizontally. This is one of 'the beautiful names of God'. The signature inscription reads 'written by Abd (the servant) Yusha' whose name is present in the Arabic seal. The Chinese seal is at present unread.
VP

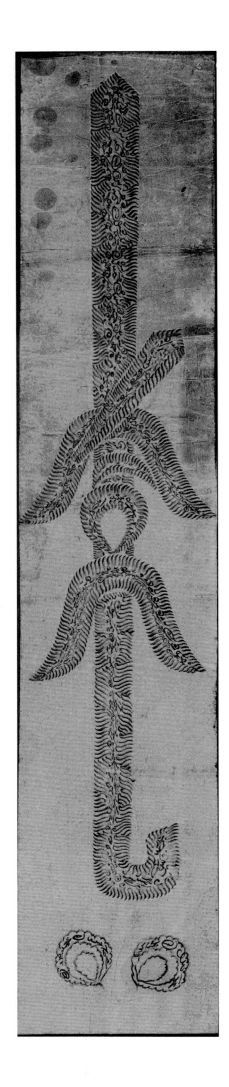

63.
Chinese Muslim scroll
China
19th century
1998.3.8

In the form of a sword, part of the word *"You who fulfill promises"* springs high in a vertical composition as if the appeal reaches up to God. This scroll is one of a quartet all written by the same calligrapher. The calligrapher relied on the flexibility of the Arabic script in shaping his words in a sword shape and used a technique called Ghubar, meaning dust to fill in the phrases of the *Shahadah*. The *Shahadah* is one of the most commonly used phrases in Chinese Muslim calligraphy, it reveals their identity as Muslims and its letters exhibits aesthetic beauty. All through the composition, the first part of the *Shahadah* creates the outline and for the filling, the second part of the *Shahadah*, *Mohammad Rasul Allah SAW* is used. The two dots of the letter Y, are added as Chinese cloud scrolls but filled with the phrase Mohammad SAW is the Prophet of Allah. The beautiful slender composition is an important adaptation of Chinese aesthetic and religious affiliation.
HB

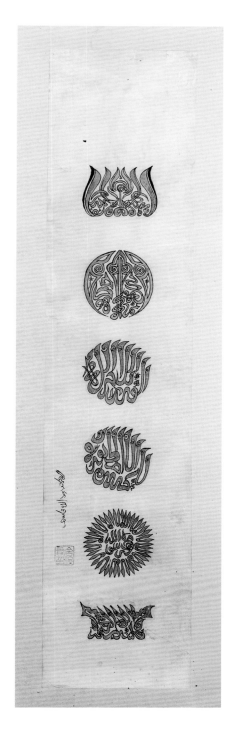

64.
Chinese calligraphic scroll
Calligrapher : Yusuf
China,
1960's
1993.3.43

In an outstanding composition, six calligraphic units are placed in a vertical alignment as if pointing up towards the creater. The lower unit is in the shape of a pot. The calligrapher has cleverly rendered the flexible curves of the Arabic letters to fit the shape. The above four roundels display in an unconventional manner four calligrapher's compositions.

The top unit is in the shape of lotus flower. The scroll has a signature at the side in red. The Chinese Muslim calligrapher created out of the Arabic calligraphy shapes that conveyed sentiments and ideas. He combined the round and geometric shapes in this composition which according to the Chinese culture formulates completeness and fulfillment. Out of each roundel, he created a separate self-contained entity. Yet together they create movement and strength. It is believed that for each unit the artist should have one breath, from the time the brush touches the scroll to the end of the phrase.
HB

65.
Chinese Muslim calligraphic scroll
Calligrapher : Shi Jen'you
China
1980 AD
1998.3.46

This horizontal composition of a Chinese Arabic calligraphic scroll introduces the *sini* Arabic script characteristic to northwest China. The central calligraphic unit represents the first Ayah of the first *surah* of the Qur'an: *"In the name of Allah, the Compassionate, the Merciful"*. At the four corners, decorative calligraphic compositions repeat the phrase *"Thank God"* in mirror images. They are depicted as butterflies, a motif popular within the Chinese ornamental vocabulary.1

Two red stamps at the left of the scroll written in Chinese script identify the calligrapher as Shi Jen'you. Chinese calligraphers

used brushes similar to those used for Chinese writings rather than reed pens. With these brushes and dark ink, they have contributed outstanding compositions in the world of Islamic calligraphy.

1. Butterflies from the 19th century Qing dynasty textiles, D'Addetta, 1981, p. 47.
HB

66.
Chinese Muslim calligraphic scroll
Calligrapher : Shi Jen'you
China
1980 AD
1998.3.36

This outstanding composition of well composed Arabic calligraphy takes the form of a Chinese blue and white dish elevated on a four footed wooden base. The Arabic letters are carefully woven into the nine peaches, representing generosity and good fortune. The dish is further decorated with Arabic verses and roundels, while on the base of the wooden stand, are the words: *God Loves the generous*. Chinese Muslim scrolls reveal the harmonious merge between the Chinese national identity and their religious affiliation.

In this beautiful composition a relationship between the meaning of the words and the symbolic image is expressed. The concept of giving ornaments meaning is characteristic to Chinese design.
HB

67a.

67b.

67c.

67d.

19th century coins, China, Brunei and Malaysia

These coins demonstrate the effect of the spread of Islam on the local cultures of China and Southeast Asia. While they maintain the shape and style of local currencies such as the Chinese *cash* coins, they include Arabic script, and as with the gold coins of *Kashgar*, strikingly beautiful *nasta'liq* calligraphy. [1]

1. Cribb et. al 1990: 194

67a.
**Bronze coin struck at
Kucha, Chinese Turkestan
in 1864**
2.5 cm (diam.), 6.4 g
BM.1902,0608.186

The form of this coin is typical
of Chinese *cash* coinage. With
its central square hole it
enabled the coins to be carried
in strings. It was struck by
Ghazi Rashid, a Muslim ruler
based at Kucha (1863-67),
who headed a major revolt
against the Chinese empire
until his death. His name
appears in Arabic on the
obverse, with the Turkish title
of *Khan* and the date, year 2
of his reign (1864). The
reverse has the mint name
described as *Dar Al-Salatana*,
'The house of the Sultanate',
the epithet for *Kucha*.

67b.
**Gold *tilla* struck at
Kashgar, Xinjiang, China,
1292/1875**
2.1 cm (diam.), 3.52 g
BM. BMC 245

This coin, known as a *tilla*
(corruption of the Indian
weight *tola* – the coin is also
known as *ashrafi*) was struck
by Ya'qub Beg (1864-77) who
headed Ghazi Rashid's revolt
in Eastern Turkestan until he
was eventually defeated and
killed by the Chinese in 1877.
This was the focus of Islamic
aspirations in this part of the
Chinese empire which were
recognized by the Ottoman
Sultan Abd Al-Aziz (1861-76)
whose name appears on the
obverse of the coin. On the
reverse is the mint, *Kashgar*,
'The house of the Sultanate'
(*Dar Al-Salatana* in Arabic in
the cursive *nasta'liq* script).

67c.
**Tin coin, *pitis* struck in the
Brunei Sultanate (Borneo),
19th century**
3.7 cm (diam.), 8.05 g
BM.1937,0704.4

This anonymous tin *pitis* has
on the obverse a traditional
mythical animal typical of
coins of this region, possibly a
dragon, and on the reverse
the Arabic inscription, *Sultan
Al-'Adil Malik Al-Zahir*, 'The
Just Sultan, the Visible King',
titles that had been used by
Muslim sultans since the
medieval period. This follows a
coin type that had circulated in
Malaysia from the end of the
18th century.

67d.
**Tin coin, *pitis* struck in the
Malay state of Patani,
1309/1891-92**
2.55 cm (diam.), 3.34 g
1921,0102.5

This tin coin shows an
interesting mix of the use of
both Arabic language and
script. While the obverse
indicates in perfect Arabic the
date and the mint, *fi bilad Al-
Patani*, 'in the country of
Patani', the reverse has an
inscription in Malay language
but in Arabic script which
reads *Ini Pitis Belanja Raja
Patani*, 'this *pitis* is the
currency of the Raja of Patani'.

68a.

68a.

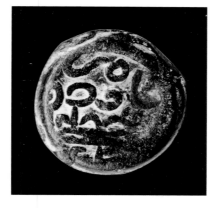
68b.

68b.

68.
Two Coins from the Melaka Sultanate
1400-1511
Melaka, Malay Peninsular

68a.
A tin cash coin of Sultan Muzaffar Shah
Melaka Sultanate, the Malay Peninsula
1445-1450 AD

The Malay world emerged as an important destination in the trade routes between East and West. The Chinese merchants and the Muslim Arab traders converged on the peninsula to conduct barter trade as early as the 7th century AD. With the rise of the Melaka Sultanate (1400-1511), gold dust, silver bars and tin blocks were used for trade. The first known minted Islamic coin was produced in the name of Sultan Muzaffer Shah (1445-1450). Minted in tin, it included on its reverse side *"the helper of the world and the religion of Islam."* Soon the Peninsula's coins incorporated the Jawi language reserving the Arabic language to religious messages. The Jawi, on the other hand used the Arabic characters.

Calligraphy minted on coins issued during the Islamic rules developed as the earliest means of self-expression and communication. Accordingly Islamic messages were transferred through coins to the followers and western allies. Verses from the Qur'an as the *Shahadah* occupied the obverse sides of coins perhaps up to the modern period, while the name of rulers, date and place of minting as well as the loyalty to Amir Al Mu'mineen (Vicegerent of the faithful),was minted on the reverse side.

68b.
A tin cash coin of Sultan Mansur Shah bin Sultan Muzaffar Shah
Melaka, the Malay Peninsula
1459-1477 AD

Similar to his father, Sultan Mansur Shah minted a tin coin on his name on the obverse side, repeating the phrase *"protector of the religion and the sultanate"*. The calligraphy exaggerates the round letters, and elongates the vertical letters of the *naskh* script. Though it is clear and decipherable, no date nor mint place is indicated.
HB

69.
An octagonal gold coin
Johor, the Malay Peninsula
1528-1564 AD

From Johor, octagonal gold minted by sultan Alauddin Riayat Shah I (1528-1564) had his name on the obverse side, while the reverse side was the phrase: "khalifat Al Mu'minin" Vicegerent of the faithful.

In the Malay world the usage of coins with Arabic inscriptions were reserved to commercial use within the states. In time Johor became a preferred trade destination over Melaka. Sultan Abdul Jalil Shah II traded directly using his own shipping fleet with merchants from Bengal, India. Yet the most widely used gold coin in Johor was the Achinese Sultan Alauddin Riayat Shah II.
HB

70.
A *kijang* Gold coin
Kelantan, the Malay Peninsula
19th century

Gold coins found in most of the Malay world do not bear a date. On one side this *kijang* shows an animal bull figure revealing his long tail, curved horns and open mouth. This *kijang* gold coin had on the reverse side few characters in Arabic indicating the words Al Adil; (the Just king). Gold coins from the Pattani and Acheh kingdoms reached most of the states of the peninsula, when Sultan Iskandar Shah (1607-1636) of Acheh aimed at enlarging his territory by incorporating Pahang, Kedah and Perak.
HB

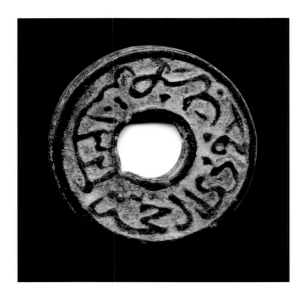

71.
Tin coins with a circular hole
Kelantan, the Malay Peninsula
1321 H/1903
20 mm

The coin was issued during the reign of Sultan Muhammad SAW IV (1889-1920) in Kelantan. Towards the end of the Sultan's reign, the central hole was omitted. The central hole of the coin, which was made for stringing, was changed in order to increase the weight of metal without increasing its size. Similar tin coins with circular holes appeared in different parts of the peninsula, in Kedah, they were called *Tra*, meaning the stamp, a word coming from the sanskrit or Thai language.
HB

Tin coin trees were popular in Kelantan, where small *pitis* were cast as petals branching off a branch. Some trees held up to 13 round coins, they were broken off when used and reassembled at later periods. Coin trees were cast in a wooden mould, introduced by the Chinese it as early as the Tang dynasty (618-906 AD). The mould for the coin tree consisted of two units, each impressed with a design. The double moulds were held together by corner pegs and clamps, and the molten metal was poured in through the bottom opening.

The coin tree shows from the obverse side the date to be *Dhul Hijja*, 1321 H/1903 AD. On the reverse side, the value (10 *pitis*) and mint place (Kelantan) were mentioned.

Two types of coin trees were known in the Malay Peninsula. HB

The Art of the Calligrapher

A well known treatise by Qadi Ahmad Ibn Mir-Munshi (d.1606) provides a wonderful and detailed description of all the calligraphers known to him, who they trained with, and what particular script they excelled at. Of the great Iraqi calligrapher Yaqut Al-Musta'simi (d.1296, who, when the Mongols attacked Baghdad, fled into a minaret with only ink and pen – with no paper – and wrote a magnificent inscription on linen) he wrote:

'In the art of writing he followed the tradition of Ibn Al-Bawwab but in the trimming of the qalam and the clipping of its nib he altered the manner of earlier masters while he drew his guidance from His Holiness the Shah, namely 'Cut the qalam so that its point be long and leave it thick; cut the end of the qalam at an angle, after which it should ring like a Mashriqi's sword'. And this Mashriqi they say was a man who made sword blades known for their excellence and quality; when blade struck something, it the blade, it vibrated a ring extreme acuteness. Therefore it is best that the end of the qalam should be cut at an angle, and the point of the qalam be long and fleshy, and when it is put to paper it should vibrate and a ringing be heard.' [1]

Images of the pen were used by Sufi writers, for example, Jalal Al-Din Al-Rumi' wrote: 'My heart is like the pen in your hand – from you comes my joy and my despair'. [2]

The association between the act of writing and Islam gave a particular status to the calligrapher. The process of acquiring proficiency in these scripts was, however, an arduous one. The calligrapher, (*khattat*), would start his studies at an early age, and was taught by a recognised master who himself may have been part of a chain of calligraphers going back to the Prophet's cousin and son-in-law Ali Ibn Abi Talib (d. 661), well known for his good hand.

The contemporary Iraqi calligrapher Ghani Alani (see Cat. no. 110) evocatively describes how he became interested in calligraphy at the age of twelve. While working on the railways to earn money, he would escape whenever he could and pick up whatever he could find by way of rough pieces of paper or card on which he would trace letters with the black of the locomotive soot. In the evenings and at weekends he would study books on calligraphy in earnest. This continued until he met the man who was to become his *ustadh* (master), Al-Khattat Hashem Muhammad Al-Baghdadi, who came from a recognised line of Iraqi calligraphers. Recalling his first meeting with his future master, Ghani Alani recounts being impressed by the sight of the wealth of masterpieces in his studio, the number of pens and the coloured inks. The master asked him

'What do you want to do with calligraphy? Do you want to write in thuluth script, that which is used for architecture and manuscripts which will open you up to universal knowledge, or would you prefer to choose the style of riqa' which will enable you to become a painter of letters?

I knew I had to make a difficult decision: was I going to content myself with learning calligraphy for utilitarian ends or was I going to place myself in the service of a master and to have to continually prove myself? I chose the latter and was put to the test. At the end of three months, my master decided that my commitment was total and decided to keep me. For the first three years of my apprenticeship, I did nothing but trace the letters of the alphabet.' [3]

The relevance of the master's question is twofold. Firstly that he clearly only wanted to teach someone intent on achieving the greatest heights of calligraphy. Secondly, it highlights the fact that while the apprentice calligrapher had to learn and become proficient in all the scripts, calligraphers became known for perfecting particular styles.

The calligrapher might study for years until he or she (there are a number of well known women calligraphers) was ready to receive his diploma, the *ijaza,* which literally means 'permission', without which he was not allowed to sign his work. The text of Ghani Alani's *ijaza* from Hashem Al-Baghdadi begins as follows:

'In the name of God the Merciful the Compassionate, who made us swear by the pen, who taught us the secrets of writing and the depths of the wisdom which has contributed to our knowledge of kingdoms and nations.
When it appeared to us that the owner of this beautiful *ijaza* had encompassed the meaning of the different styles, reaching a degree of

total perfection, I gave him permission to place his name on beautiful writings....'[4]

This section of the exhibition concentrates on the art of the calligrapher and included here are examples of the tools of the trade such as the reed pens, scissors and blades, pen-boxes and ink-wells. Traditionally calligraphers made their own ink. One ink (*midad*) was made from soot mixed with a binder of gum Arabic, and dissolved in water. Other colours such as walnut cordial could be added to make a rich brown. The ink is mixed in an ink-well containing threads of silk. These protect the pen from knocking against the edges of the ink-well. Another traditional type of ink known as *hibr* is more metallic and includes nut gall (an excrescence produced by a parasite on an oak tree) added to either metallic salts such as vitriol, alum or sulphates with, as before, the gum arabic to bind it. [5] Nowadays, many calligraphers use commercially produced inks. Ghani Alani is one of the exceptions (see Cat. no. 110).

The calligrapher puts on his glasses, and indulges in a mystical experience. Letters after letters, words over the other forming lines of blackened composition from the practice sheets. The sheets, known as *Siyah Mashq*, reveal the mystical compositions of the Arabic letters. (Cat. no. 86)

1. Minorsky 1959: 57-8
2. Schimmel 1990: 87
3. Alani and Meffre 2002: 19 (these passages are translated from French by the author)
4 Alani and Meffre 2002: 19
5. Guesdon et. al 2001: 23; Derman 1998

73.
Riza, Drawing of a
calligrapher, Isfahan, Iran,
c. 1600
10 cm x 7 cm
BM.1920,0917.0271 (1)

The calligrapher is about to start writing, an open book in his hand, his round ink-well and pens by his side. The painting [1] is signed by this well known Persian painter with the words *'Riza drew it'* and it also bears a seal of the Safavid Shah of Iran Abbas I (1588-1629) who evidently had this in his library. The seal is inscribed, *'Abbas the servant of the king of holiness'*. The chronicler of Persian painters and calligraphers, Qadi Ahmad, wrote of Riza as follows : '...*he brought the elegance of his brushwork, portraiture, and likeness to such a degree that, if Mani and Behzad (earlier celebrated Iranian painters)* *were living today, they would praise his hand and brush a hundred times a day'* [2]

1. Canby 1996: 184; Adamova 2000: 33
2. Minorsky 1959: 37
VP

168

74.
Cylindrical cast brass ink-well inlaid with silver, **Khorasan, eastern Iran/Afghanistan, late 12th–early 13th century**
9.8 cm (height)
BM.1939,0620.1

The inscriptions in angular *kufic* and the cursive *naskh* scripts consist of good wishes to an unnamed owner, *'Perpetual glory, honour, dominion, good fortune, peace and long life to its owner'*. [1]

The medieval writer Qalqashandi refers to the ink-well (*dawayah*) as 'the mother of all tools' and a scribe without his *dawat* is compared to 'a man who enters a fight without a weapon'.[2] Cylindrical ink-wells –originally in glass - were recommended because dirt and powder did not accumulate in them and they could easily be cleaned. According to religious sensibilities because of the relationship between the art of writing and God, some Muslim writers prohibited the use of ink-wells and pen-boxes made of precious metals and recommended the avoidance of figural decoration on them – proscriptions which were clearly disregarded at certain times.

1. Barrett 1949: ix; Ward 1993: 15
2. Baer 1983: 68
VP

75.
Cast brass writing box,
India, late 19th century
30 cm (length)
BM.1996,0223.1

This is made of two separate tubular pen holders and a cylindrical ink-well in the shape of an onion dome commonly found in the Mughal and later architecture of India.
VP

76.
Rectangular brass pen-box
with rounded ends inlaid
with silver and gold,
probably Syria c. 1300-50.
22.2 cm (length)
BM.1881,0802.19

Inside the pen-box[1] are two compartments: the larger one for pens, the smaller for the ink. The decoration on the lid and inside the box consists of a series of seated figures within roundels either holding goblets, playing musical instruments or in other poses. Around the sides is a fretwork pattern with alternating squares of facing ducks and geometric designs.

1.Barrett 1949 :xv
VP

**77.
Lacquer pen-box, Iran,
19th century**.
**23.5 cm (length)
BM.OA+7410**

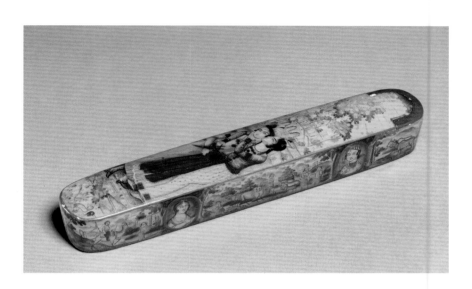

Made from *papier-maché* painted and varnished, pen-boxes such as these, bearing designs akin to Persian miniature painting, were made in Iran. A major centre was Isfahan. [1] The design on the top of the pen-box consists of a couple standing in a landscape by a river; buildings and a bridge are in the background. Around the sides are rural scenes with animals, a series of portraits, and a veiled woman being led by a man on a camel.

1. Khalili et. al. 1996: 10, 54
VP

**78.
Collection of pens and a
sand container
11-26 cm (length)
OA+ 14021, 14027, 14029,
14030; 2003,0322.1-4
(presented by Nassar
Mansour)
Qasr Ibrim pens : Egypt
Exploration Society**

The pen (*qalam*) used by Muslim calligraphers was almost always made of reed, although nowadays many calligraphers use metallic nibs. Strict rules were laid down in calligraphic treatises about the type of reed to be employed and the angles at which they should be cut. These practises are still used by traditional calligraphers today. The *qalam* had to be both solid and pliable. The traditional method to cut the reed is as follows: When the reed is dry, it is placed in the palm of the hand and cut with a knife until it is in the shape of an almond. It is then re-cut to the desired width, which altered with the thickness depending on the size and type of script to be practised. The nib was then slit, which enabled the ink to flow regularly. [1] With extensive use the nib had frequently to be re-cut, as it wore easily, shortening the pen. Included here are a number of reed pens of different periods: 19th century unused decorated Ottoman examples, three examples with ink on their nibs from the site of Qasr Ibrim in Nubia (present-day Sudan and a military outpost of the Ottoman Empire until 1812), and some modern pens that show different stages in the cutting of the pen. Sand was sprinkled onto the ink to help it dry.

1. Derman 1998: 7-9
VP

172

79.
An Ottoman silver
scribe's set
Turkey
18th century
26.6 cm
2003.6.2

The silver scribe's set consisting of a pen case and attached inkwell is an important part of the calligrapher's tools. This silver case and inkwell have hinged covers decorated from the rim area by a continuous floral design. The Ottoman sultan's *Tughra* and the maker's mark were impressed on the case. The *Tughra* appears twice, at the bottom of the inkwell and on the side of the pen case. The *Tughra* indicates the reign of Sultan Abdul Majid II (1839 –1861 AD).

An emblem indicating the name of the craftsmen such as Wahbi was stamped near the ink case lid. The positioning of the maker's mark was usually found at the upper side of the case near the lid. Wahbi was a known craftsman who signed other inkwells and cases during the periods of Sultan Abdulmejid (1839–1861 AD) and Sultan Abdulaziz (1861-1876 AD).

1. Kurkman, 1996, p.109.
HB

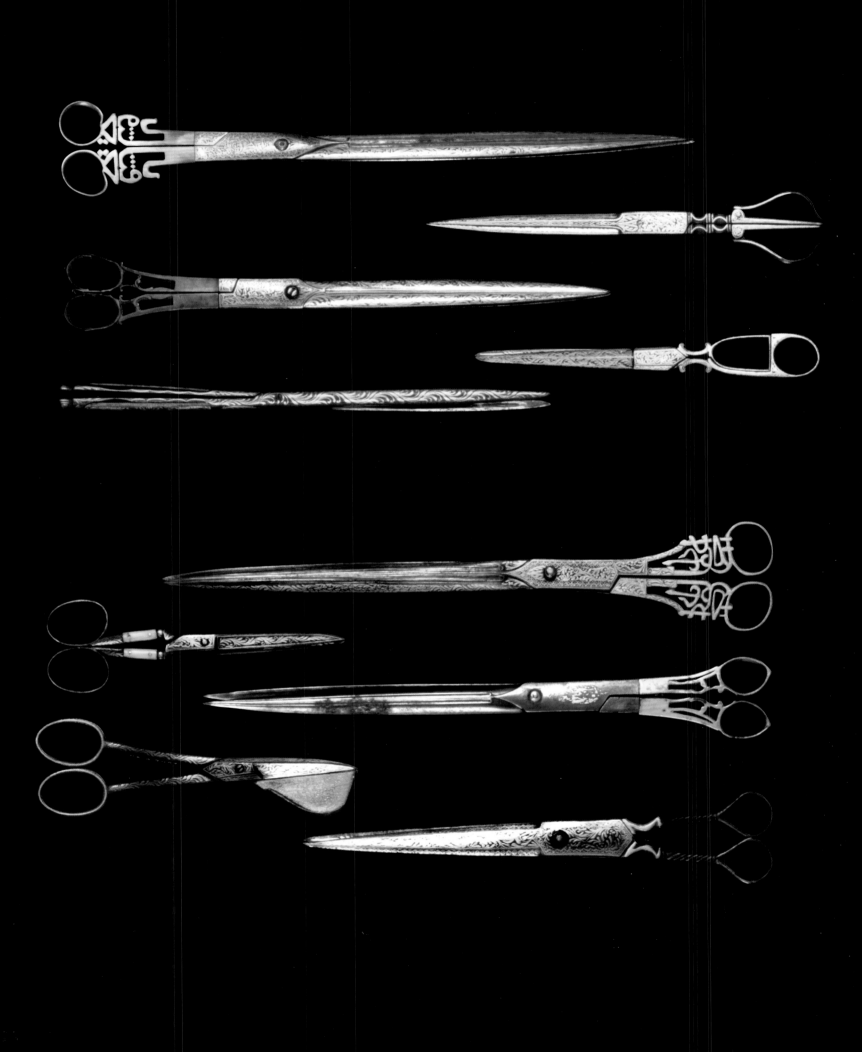

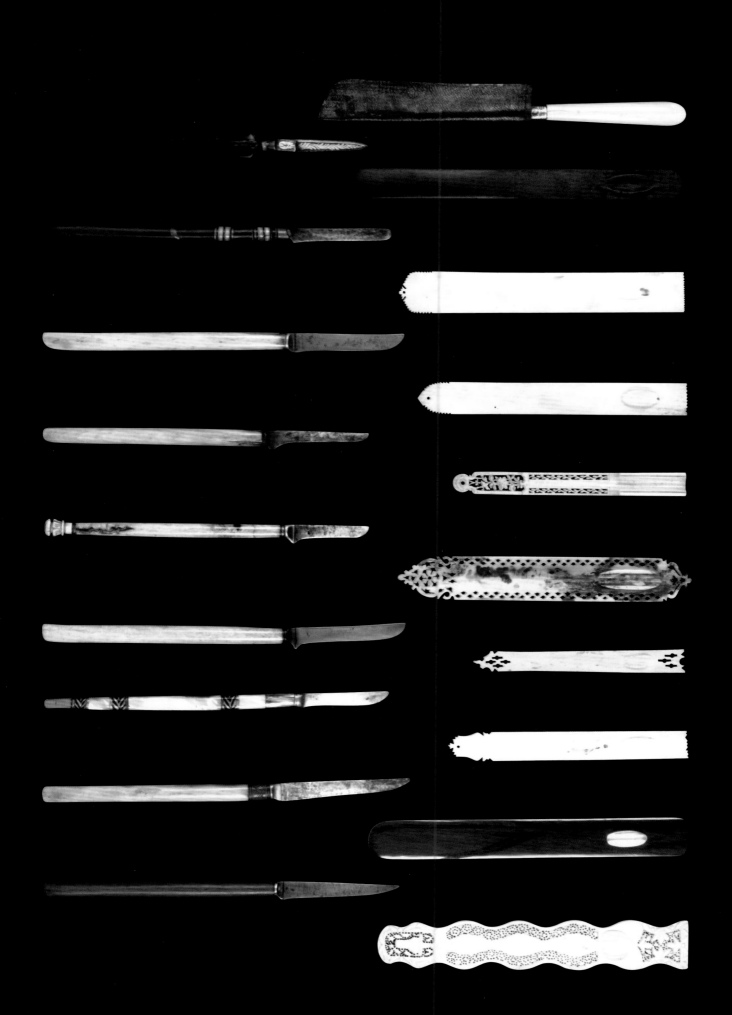

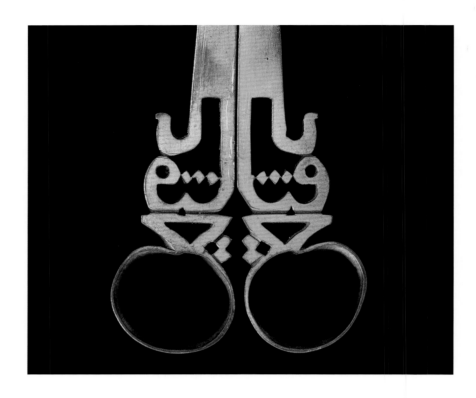

80.
A collection of Ottoman calligrapher's tools
Istanbul, Turkey
19th century
2002.6.24-52

The collection comprises of 10 pairs of various damascened steel scissors with gold scrolling floral designs, one blade with side tray, 10 knives for trimming quills with decorated handles and 9 pen-rests made of ivory, dark jade and ebony with pierced designs.

The scissors form a unique collection as they display various forms of handles and ring grips, different sizes and different decorations. In the collection of 10 shears, one pair of scissors has a single round handle for a single finger, another has an adjustable grip for the fingers, and two display mirror imaged calligraphic words: *Ya Fattah*; "the Opener" one of the 99 names of God. This phrase is commonly used on 18th and 19th century shears found at the Topkapi Palace Museum and Sadberk Hanim Museum in Turkey. The shears are all embellished with gold thread in relief in dense leaf scroll motifs (*koftagari* technique). The shears were used to trim paper, create *muraqqa'* folios for albums and in book binding. The scissor with the side tray and raised handles was used to smooth the surface of papers and reduce the gum or wax placed on them so as to allow for proper ink absorption. All the scissors are made of steel.

The pen rests were called the *Makta'* and their function was to hold the reed pens in place while the nib was cut, as well as while the calligrapher rests. Accordingly the size of these instruments may change indicating the type of reed for which they were made for. The collection displays a variety of

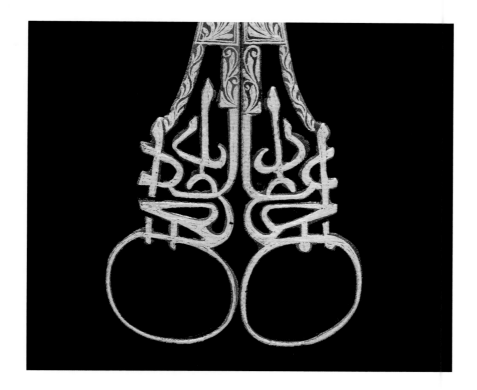

decorations, ranging from simple plain pen rests, to highly ornate pierced and wavy edges.

A unique ivory pen rest (2002.6.26) displays a *Mewlevi* headgear in relief in the piercing technique. The depiction of such a headgear indicates that the user was associated with the Dervish orders. Ivory, walrus tusk, tortoiseshell and mother of pearl were smooth yet hard materials that were favourably used for *Makta's*. These materials would not damage the blade of the cutter when trimming the nibs.

A collection of 10 knives is mostly composed of steel blades and ivory handles. The steel blades were always razor sharp, and in many cases stamped with the master craftsmen's signature, which in time wore out. The handles in many cases vary from plain to highly decorative ivory, mother of pearls, jade, quartz or wood, and in other cases are adorned with metal threads and semi-precious stones such as coral. The handles are usually hollow and in some cases they contain a smaller blade. From the collection, several of the blades have a tear drop stamp common in 19th century Ottoman knives found at the Topkapi Palace Museum, while only one blade is adorned with floral motifs in gold thread.

To the calligrapher, his tools were as important as his fingers. And through them, he could best fulfil his duty - to beautify the Word of God.
HB

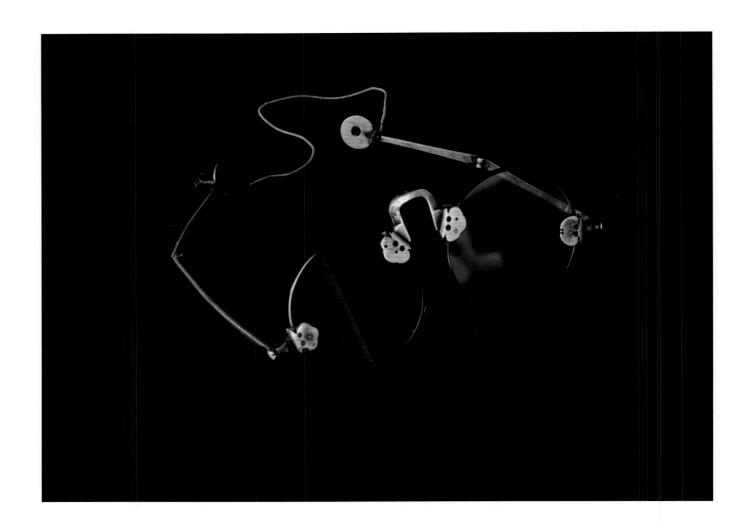

81.
Calligrapher's Spectacles
China, 19th–20th century
AD
1998.3.52

Miniatures depicting calligraphers with spectacles appeared in Iran during the Safavid period (1501-1722 AD). Yet in China, the earliest excavated crystal glasses date from the East Han Dynasty (25–220 AD), and the famous Ming Dynasty (1368-1644) writer and calligrapher Zhu Zhishan was known to have possessed magnifying glasses. In 1270 and during his journey to China, Marco Polo observed the elderly Chinese using spectacles. From the Muslim world, the Arab scientist Ibn Al Heitham (965-1039 AD) discussed the feasibility of the magnification by crystal planes as an aid for weak eyesight. The Chinese themselves claim that spectacles originated in Arabia in the 11th century and the lenses were made of polished jade and crystal.
HB

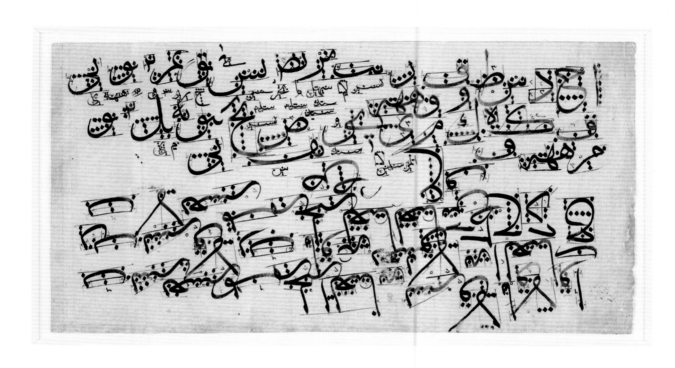

82.
Calligraphic exercise,
Ottoman Turkey, c. 18th-
19th century
12.2 cm x 23.8 cm
BM.2003,027.01
Presented by Oliver Hoare

The student of calligraphy working with a recognized master, had to demonstrate his or her proficiency in all the canonical scripts, a process that could take many years, in order to obtain the diploma – the *ijaza* -which then allowed the calligrapher to practise and teach. In particular the calligrapher had to demonstrate his ability to control the proportions of the letter forms because this lay at the heart of the art of calligraphy as laid down by the great master Ibn Muqla in the 9th century and followed thereafter. This exercise, [1] which is unsigned but shows the influence of the well known Turkish calligrapher Mustafa Rakim (d.1826), [2] is in two styles – *naskh* and *thuluth* – and shows each letter with a series of rhombic dots next to it that provided the framework for the creation of the shapes. It is inscribed with a phrase often set by the master as an exercise for his students: *'Oh Lord make it easy and not difficult, oh Lord may it be completed in the best way'.* [3]

1.Hoare 1987:2; for other examples see Derman 1998: 154;
2. This was suggested to the author by Nassar Mansour. For examples of the calligraphy of Mustafa Rakim see Derman 1998: 98ff
3. For an example of this phrase on an exercise by Sevki Efendi see Derman 1998: 126
VP

دُونِ اللَّهِ مَا لَا
يَمْلِكُ لَكُمْ ضَرًّا
وَلَا نَفْعًا وَاللَّهُ

جز خدای آنچ راكه نه
كه
توانند مشما را گزند كردن
سود كردن
ونه سود كردن وخدای

83.
**Qur'an page, coloured inks
and water colour on paper,
Iran, Anatolia or Northern
India, 14th century
29 cm x 18.5 cm
BM.1993,1009.01**

Double-page from the Qur'an chapter 5: 75-77 inscribed with three lines of *muhaqqaq* script with interlinear Persian translation and pious sayings in angular script within the illumination. Styles of script that demonstrate the ability of this calligrapher in three script styles are evident here: the *muhaqqaq* script of the

Qur'anic text, *naskh* for the Persian translation, and the angular archaic *kufic* style for the pious sayings around the margin. There has been some debate about the history of this now dispersed Qur'an that centres on its unusual and striking marginal decoration. While the main script and the Persian translations suggest

an eastern Islamic source, an Indian connection has been suggested for the style of the illumination. An alternative Anatolian provenance has also been put forward. [1]

1. James 1988, Cat. no. 60 for pages from the same Qur'an.
VP

83a
**Album of c. 17th-19th
century miniatures and
calligraphic spcimens
within ornate Qajar
persian mid 19th century
lacquer bookcovers
18.7 x 25 cm
194,0617.03
Image page 18**

Albums made up of individual miniatures or calligraphies were popular in Iran and elsewhere from about the 15th century. Collectors who could not afford to commission complete manuscripts would acquire

single miniatures, sketches or virtuosi examples f calligraphy from their favourite artists and put them together like a scrapbook. This album includes a number of pages of calligraphy in many different styles, pasted onto colourred card and made up into a book. the page displayed which is unsigned is in Turkish style in a format developed by the well known Turkish calligrapher Shaykh Hamdullah (d. 1520). Two styles of script thuluth and naskh have been used to write one of the sayings of the Prophet Muhammad SAW.

علي الصفحة احسن فا دا
فصده عن الغبار في اواني
خر في حل الذهب ترقّقه وتقرّضه
عله فيه فاذا احمر الذهب
يين عبد ونصوطه وتقلبه
فاذا رابته خشن الجسمه
صلايه نظّفه والاف اعد
ببغ الي ان يستقيم وثم
ته في ذبيق الاكثا من
ه هشته اجزا عبد واقله
بين ذلك فهو سهل الماخذ
وهذا الما يحمر الصفيحه
كالعادة فاذا المرت بلغ المقصود
اعد عليها العمل فاذا احمرت
قبل ان تركب عليها الزببق
الطلا معروف يد رك بالعيان
خوف الاطالة فاذا اطلبت
وطبيرت

وطبيرت العبد ومكثت الشمس علي الشغل رمله اولا
بالرمل الناعم وجففه بخرقة وا صقله بصقلة
بولاد منعمة مثل للجزع بريقك الي ان يبرضيك
لمعنته ثم امسحه بقطنة نظيفة صحا قويا وحره
الي ان ترضيك حمرته وقد تقدم ما تذهيب
النحاس الاحمر تجرده وتنعمه بالسنباذج او المسن
وتغسله بالنوشاد والمحلول في الخل واللم رطبر
ويكون مسحوق معهما قليل زبيق ونضربهم
في خرقته وتغمسها في الخل و تدعك لها الصفيحه
الي ان تنبيض وتركب عليها العبد ثم اغسلها
وجففها بخرقة وركب عليها الذهب المحلول
كما فعلت بالحد يد والحد ر في التطيير عنه وعن
غيره من كثرة النار اياك ان تري الذهب بينفل
علي الشغل وتتركه بل خذه عن النار بسرعة ثم
امسحه بالخرقة الرفيعة النظيفه واعده قليلا
قليلا الي ان يطير بالتدريج فا فعل به ما يليق
من الترميل والصقل الي ان بينتهي واما تذهيب

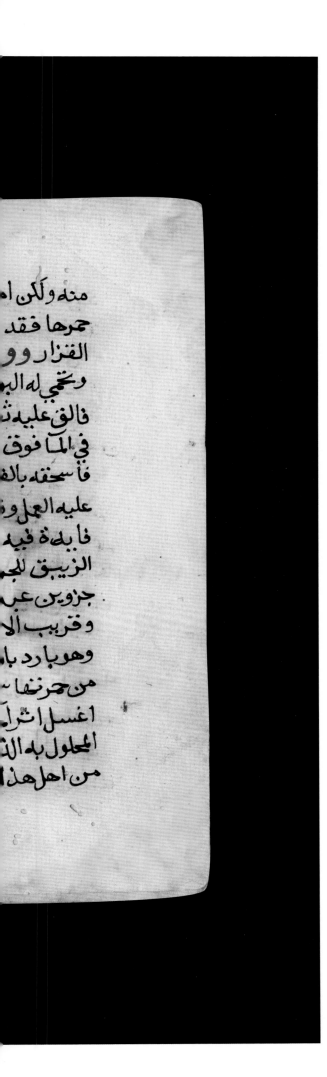

84.
The Bright Stars Ottoman Treatise
Damascus, Syria
940 H/1545 AD
20.0 cm x 13.5 cm
2002.1.168

The book of the Spider web; *kitab Nasj Al Inkabut*; volume entitled The Bright Stars; *Kitab Al Nujum Al Shariqat fi Zikr Ba'd Al Sanayi'* is a treatise produced in 940 H/1545 AD, and is composed and inscribed by Shaykh Ibn Abi Al Khayr Al Husayni al Damashqi. The treatise is divided into 25 chapters; *babs*, all dealing with colour, colour mixtures, pigments from stones, gold and silver. Instructions on how to prepare pigments and apply them on different media as ivory, bones, wood or paper have also been explained.

The document is inscribed in a simple black *riqqa'* script, with headings in red, and dark brown leather binding which includes a central medallion decorated with saz leaves. This in turn supports that the production of this treaties was in Damascus during the Ottoman rule.

The right folio reveals the secrets of gilding used for illuminations. *"if you want to test it, do so by placing the fixture on a paper, if it leaves red stains, then it is ripe and protect it from dust in glass containers. Another factor concerning gold, its beating and texture, if gold becomes red then add to it double its weight of ABD and stir it with water. If on the paper its consistency is still rough, then re heat it in a clean container, rework on it and add to it…"* The left folio recalls the method to produce gilded copper. *"Gilding the red copper requires that you grind it and create a smooth texture out of it, wash carefully and dilute with vinegar, then add a little mercury and beat. Submerge a cloth in vinegar and rub the surface till it becomes white. Wash and dry before applying the gold surface. Beware not to let the gold evaporate due to the extra heat…"*

Treaties as such can be considered a treasure for calligraphers, who acquired the secrets of preparing pigments and know the problems related to dyes on paper and on different media, from their teachers.
HB

85.
A calligrapher's letter
Calligrapher : Dervish
Abdul Majid Taleghani
Date : 1757-1771
Style : *Shikasteh*
16.7 cm x 9.3 cm
1998.2.71

The letter was written by Dervish Abdul Majid Taleghani to his friend calligrapher Mirza Abdul Wahab. The folio depicts eight horizontal lines, upside down phrases and corner words within cloud shaped compartments against a gold ground. The calligraphy moves up and around framing the folio. The folio is mounted on a board with polychrome floral boarder.

The text mentions the period of the execution of the folio to be at the end of the month of Ramadan, and the purpose was to inform his friend that he will not be able to complete a document. Abdul Majid accordingly recommends that the friend (as a sign of great confidence in his skillful hand) finishes the job. Abdul Majid further adds that some of the calligraphy folios he has collected became wet and have been destroyed.

A century later, Dervish Abdul Majid Taleghani (1185/1741-2) became the master of the *shekasteh* style. Dervish Abdul Majid in numerous folios gives himself the title of *shekasteh nigar* or the *shekasteh* writer. The *shekasteh* script developed out of *nasta'liq*. It had a set of complex rules, in which shorthand like symbols were employed. In time the rules were disregarded and more freedom was given to the artist for independent expression.

The *shekasteh* script described as the broken script developed and flourished in Iran during the 16th/17th century. It is an elegant yet legible script that appears broken as the letters joined together due to the swiftness of the calligrapher's hand. The script developed for official documents yet it became more famous as a decorative composition than for official proclamations.
HB

184

86.
A mystical single folio of
Siyah Mashq
Calligrapher : Mir Imad
Isfahan, Iran
17th century
31.0 cm x 20.5 cm
1998.2.117

The dense folio of overlapping script is the exercise work of renowned Persian calligrapher Mir Imad (d. 1615). The artist refers to the folio as a blackened page (*meswadah*) yet the composition of the script and its powerful diagonal strokes create an inspiring sense of movement. This mystical experience has attracted many viewers irrespective of its illegible text. Mir Imad proudly signs his sheets acknowledging their uniqueness and subtlety. As a young calligrapher, Mir Imad lived and worked in Qazvin. Yet shortly after settling in Isfahan, he was murdered.

Siyah Mashq or exercise sheets are an essential part of a calligrapher's written record. The calligrapher would use all available areas of the sheet for economical reasons, resulting in a steady repetition of letters and words over each other in a dense composition. HB

87.
Calligraphic page, signed
by Fakhri, Turkey c.16th
century
27 cm x 17 cm
BM.1949,1008.133

This is an example of the technique of *découpage* in which the letters are cut out with scissors and pasted onto paper. The calligraphy is in *nasta'liq* script in white with floral designs, and lies against a deep indigo ground. It is mounted on a green page. [1] The inscription consists of the invocation to *Imam* Ali : *'Call upon Ali who causes wonders to appear, you will find him a help to you in adversity, all anguish and sorrow will disappear through your friendship oh Ali, oh Ali, oh Ali.'* The signature Fakhri is short for Fakhri Ibn Vali el-Brusevi who was well known as a paper cutter. [2]

1. Safadi 1978: Fig. 89
2. Rogers and Ward 1988: 56; for another example of Fakhri's work see Hoare 1987:19
VP

y88.
Part of a letter of recommendation issued by the Shrine of *Imam* Rida at Mashad in Iran dated 14 *Dhu'l Hijja* 939/July 1533
28.8 cm x 19.5 cm (each part)
BM.1996,0521.01

This document [1] is inscribed in black, blue and gold inks in the *divani* script favoured during the 15th and 16th centuries in Iran for decrees and royal correspondence. It was issued for a person named as Darwish Khidr Shah, son of Ustad Mahmud Yazdi by the shrine that is highly revered by Shi'a Muslims as it is associated with the *Imam* Ali Al-Rida. It bears two seals,

one of which is dated 934/1527-28. The text, which is missing a number of sections, begins by praising the benefits of making the pilgrimage to Mashhad. It follows by recounting in essence that Khidr Shah has performed the rituals of pilgrimage and has spent two periods of forty days engaged in devotional exercises at the shrine during which he passed

every third night awake in prayer. As he now intends to visit the other shrines of the *imams* (these, such as Najaf and Kerbela, are in Iraq) he asked for a recommendation and this document was made in response to this request.

1. Canby 1999: 56. The document was read by Alexander Morton.
VP

89.
Calligraphic page,
Lucknow, India, mid 18th
century
9.3 cm x 10 cm
BM.1946,1010.02

The calligraphy is *nasta'liq* that is written at an angle within cloud shapes which are surrounded by delicate floral scrolls. There are blue triangles filled with flowers and a decorative border, gold on an orange ground. It is inscribed with a Persian quatrain in the larger size script which expresses dissatisfaction with the absence of peace, and recommends searching for a place where those who like to drink go to. In smaller script is the signature 'written by the guilty servant Hafiz Nurallah may God forgive his sins.' This calligrapher was in the service of the Nawab of Lucknow Asaf Al-Dawla (1774-97). [1]

1. Bayani 1966-9, 1: 949; Dihlavi 1910: 64. I am grateful to Manijeh Bayani for these references.
VP

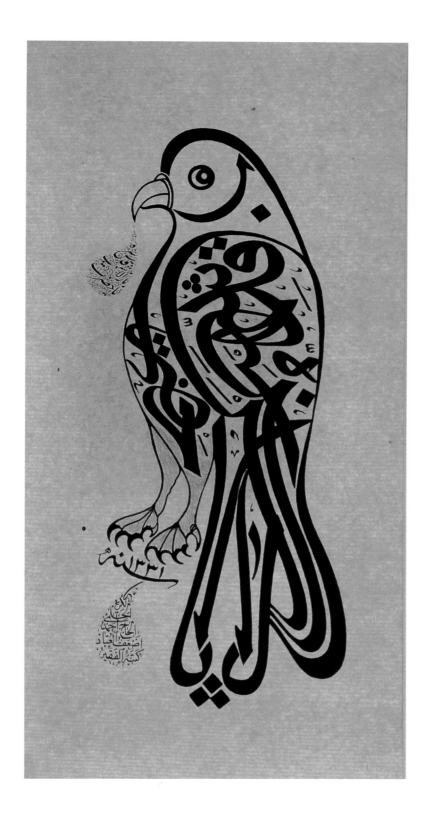

**90.
Ahmad Al-Helmi,
calligraphic bird,
1331/1912-13
47.5 cm x 23.5 cm
Private Collection**

This bird is made up of words in Arabic and Ottoman Turkish that refer to an unnamed Sufi saint who is described as a grey luminous eagle. This is followed by the phrase 'may God hallow his secret', a eulogy often uttered after the name of a deceased Muslim saint. These words form the body of the bird and also stream out of his beak. It is signed by the artist who describes himself as the poor, the humblest of servants, the *Hajj* (who has been on the pilgrimage to Mecca) Ahmad Al-Helmi. The Helmi family was a well-known Ottoman family of scribes. [1]

1. I am grateful to Nabil Saidi for this information.
VP

**91.
Gold calligraphy on red silk, Turkey, 19th century
56 cm x 91.5 cm
OA+ 0351**

This calligraphy is simply inscribed in *jali thuluth*, (a form of *thuluth* particularly practised by Ottoman calligraphers) with the phrase: *'Salvation is in truth'*. Silk as a background for calligraphic painting was particularly favoured by 19th century Ottoman calligraphers. [1]

1. See for example Derman 1998: 98
VP

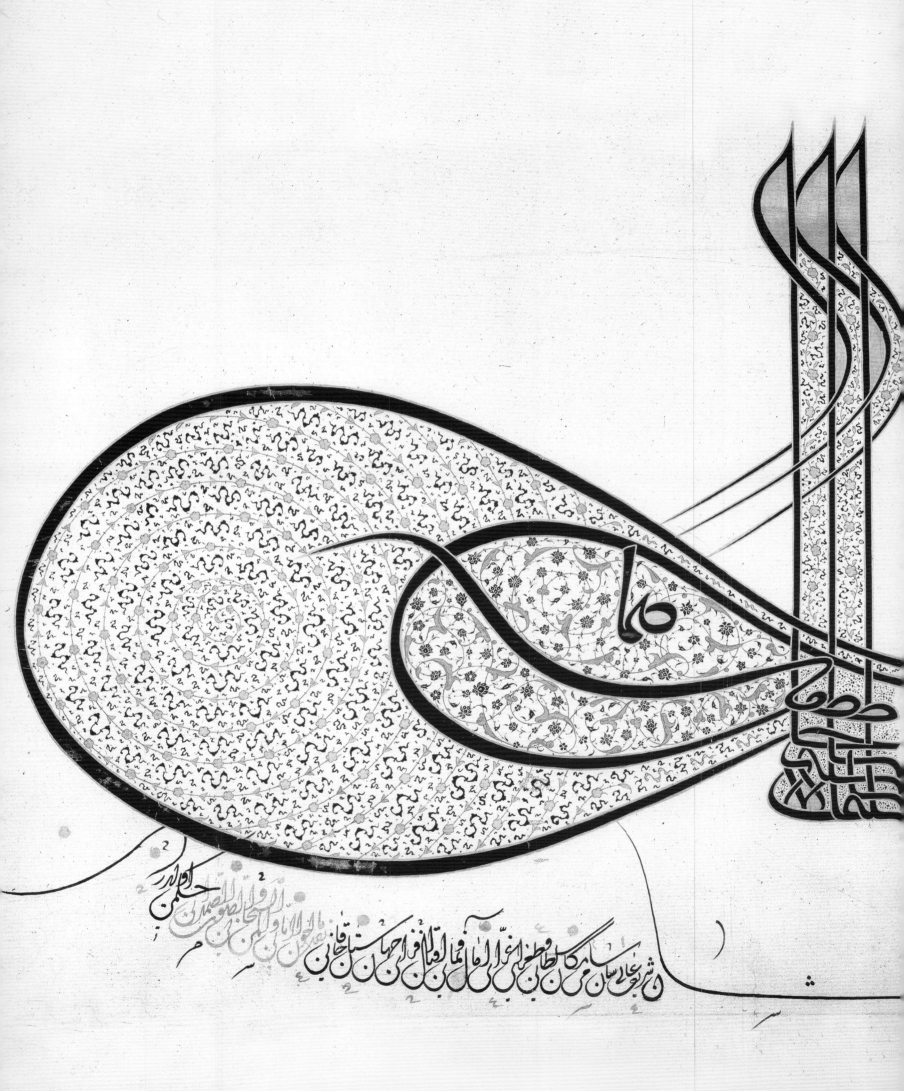

92.
***Tughra* of Sultan Suleyman the Magnificent, blue and gold inks on paper, Ottoman Turkey, 1520-66**
43.5 cm x 62 cm
BM.1949,0409.096

The *tughra* is an intricate device that served as the imperial monogram of the Ottoman sultans. In addition to its use on documents, it is also found on coins. These documents, known as *firmans* (commands) or *berat* (written documents), would have been rolled, and were issued by the *Diwan* (Council of State) on all manner of subjects concerned with the functioning of the Ottoman Empire, from relations with other states to petitions from individuals. In order to avoid forgery, the *tughra* was drawn and illuminated only when the document was ready to be dispatched. [1] It is not known what type of document this magnificent example was attached to because only the first introductory line written in the *divani* script favoured by the Ottoman chancellery survives. Beautifully illuminated, it bears the sultan's name, Suleyman Shah, and that of his father, Selim, and the phrase, 'the one who is always victorious'. [2]

1. Nadir 1986: 17-19; Rogers and Ward 1998: 56-64
2. Rogers 1983: 45
VP

The Power of the Word

This section includes a number of different kinds of objects from weapons, standards used in religious processions, protective robes, amulets, belt buckle and popular stickers you might put in the car. Each is imbued with amuletic and protective powers by virtue of the inscriptions and symbols engraved upon it. To prevent misfortune and against the evil eye, in different parts of the Muslim world people will call upon God, or revered figures in Islam and utter and inscribe favourite protective verses from the Qur'an. In battle they may wear talismanic shirts inscribed with verses from the Qur'an or use swords inscribed with 'the beautiful names of God'. To cure sickness they might drink from a magical bowl, or drink the water used when washing clean the writing boards used to learn the Qur'an, or have an amulet made by a holy man. There are myriad purposes for which such objects were made and used, their specific purpose often no longer clear to us today. Many of these objects can be termed 'magical'. But magic in this context is not malign. People believed that there were two kinds of magic: licit and illicit. According to the 10th century writer Ibn Al-Nadim, 'while licit magicians constrain the spirits by obeying and supplicating God, illicit magicians enslave the spirits by offerings and evil deeds'. [1]

1.Dodge 1970, II: 726.

93.
Ottoman Child's Robe
Turkey
18th century
49 cm x 97 cm
2002.6.19

The child's robe is made of interwoven silk fabric in cream against crimson ground. The overall composition is reminiscent to the design utilised on the black silk Kiswa (drapes of the Holy Kaaba). The design is composed of zigzag design where the *Shahadah*: the profession of faith, is inscribed in light cream. The robe buttons and edges were embroidered in metal threads while the lining of the body is in green silk and the lining of the sleeves is in yellow silk. This design was reserved for special use and this robe would have only been commissioned for a member of the royalty.

The calligraphy reveals besides the *Shahadah*, a verse from the Qur'an(2:144) and several phrases within circular and polylobed compartments that calls upon God with his attributes: *Ya Hannan* (the loving, the compassionate), *Ya Mannan* (the generous provider), and *Ya Sultan* (the king).

Such garments became popular during the 17th, 18th and 19th centuries in Ottoman Turkey. They were worn as protective garments, yet the same fabric design was used on cenotaph covers and linings. Cloth with Qur'anic verses were believed to have been worn only by the pure; children who have not reached puberty, by the deceased after their bodies have been purified, or on the Kaaba as drapes indicating its pure nature.
HB

94.
Chinese porcelain magic-medicinal bowl, 18th century
20.5 cm (diam.)
BM. F619A

A 14th century treatise asserted that 'protection against delusions and melancholia could be gained by drinking before breakfast for three days from a bowl from which Qur'anic verses and a particular magic square had been written. This Chinese bowl is based on a form of metalwork magic bowl that is common throughout the Middle-East from about the 12th century. On the two outer rings, and part of the third, verses from *Surah* II

(The Cow) verses 255-257 which continues with the *Shahadah* and invocations to God; the 4th ring invokes God with one of his 'divine names'. The 5th ring contains the invocation to Imam Ali 'Call upon Ali who makes wonders appear, you will find him a help to you in adversity, all care and grief will clear away through your prophethood oh Muhammad SAW through your friendship, oh Ali, oh Ali/oh Ali'. While around the 4 x 4 magic square in the centre is

the phrase 'there is no conqueror except for Ali, and no sword except for *Dhu'l Faqar*'. [1] These bowls are likely to have been made either for export to Iran, or for (Shi'i) Chinese Muslims.

1. A bowl with virtually identical inscriptions is published in Maddison and Savage-Smith 1997, 1 : 104. For a discussion of magic bowls and their inscriptions see Maddison and Savage-Smith 1997: 72 ff.
VP

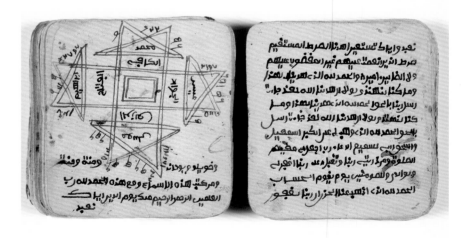

95.
Magical text, Sub-Saharan Africa, 19th century.
10 cm x 10 cm
1998,1016.02

Texts such as these, which consist of formulae for protection and that include drawings of magical squares or other elements, are widespread across the Islamic world. Many of them are based on the text of a

medieval author Al-Buni, (d. 1225), who wrote the most popular treatise on occult practice and talismans. The manuscript is cut square and is unbound but would originally have been kept in a leather bag. The style of the

script is a form of the *maghribi* script known as *sudani*. 1

1. Guesdon et al. 2001: 69; Bravmann 1983: 21
VP

96.
Osman Waqialla, _Kaf ha ya ayn sad_, ink and gold on vellum, 1980
17.5 cm x 13 cm
1998,0716.01

This calligraphic page is inscribed with Chapter 19 ('Maryam') from the Qur'an. Boldly written in _thuluth_ script are five Arabic letters (_kaf ha ya ayn sad_) that appear at the beginning of this chapter. In tiny _naskh_ script all around, the rest of the chapter in inscribed. These single letters are some of 'the mysterious letters of the Qur'an' which precede twenty-nine of the 114 chapters. They are imbued with magical protective properties and are often found engraved on amulets. Osman Waqialla was born in Rufa'a in Sudan, studied art in Britain and Sudan and trained as a calligrapher in Egypt with the master Sayyid Ibrahim. He has lived and worked in Britain since 1967.[1]

1. Seven Stories 1995: 110ff.
VP

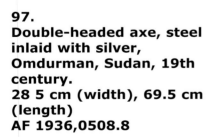

97.
Double-headed axe, steel inlaid with silver, Omdurman, Sudan, 19th century.
28 5 cm (width), 69.5 cm (length)
AF 1936,0508.8

The axe is covered with what appear to be Arabic inscriptions. But while there are some recognisable words such as 'Allah' repeated, the rest are meaningless. The shape of the axe is based on an Iranian prototype of the Qajar period of a type that might have been traded at this time. It has been suggested that such objects which were largely ceremonial may have been presented to Sudanese tribal chiefs as a token of appreciation by Arab traders. [1]

1. Spring 1993: pg. 83
VP

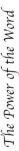

98a.

98g.

98j.

98m.

Amulets

Throughout the Islamic world, amulets are made in a variety of materials and take many forms. [1] They can be paper and placed inside amulet holders, or made from metal or semi-precious stones. They are often worn as rings or pendants, sometimes written in reverse in order to be stamped onto something, or as plaques or stickers placed in the home. The material of the amulet itself can be important with beneficiary properties attached to certain stones. Carnelian, for example, is very popular, being the stone preferred by the Prophet Muhammad SAW himself. It is often difficult to establish the date or from where in the Islamic world many of these amulets have come (if there is no corroborating evidence such as when a particular object entered the British Museum collection). The amulets are grouped according to the content of their inscription, with verses from the Qur'an first, and the more esoteric examples with signs, symbols and magical squares at the end.

VP

1. Canaan 1937 and 1938; Kalus 1981 section III.1: 70-90; Content 1987: 314 ff; Porter 1998; Porter forthcoming.

98a.
Cowrie shell inscribed in angular script with forked terminals
1.4 cm x 1 cm (irreg.)
1861,0628.34

The words inscribed here, 'Except he the living' are from Qur'an 2: 255 known as the 'throne verse'. This verse, which is written out in full on the amulet described below is known as the 'verse of seeking refuge' or the 'verse for driving out Satan' and appears in various other contexts such as inscriptions on buildings. Cowrie shells have traditionally been used in the Islamic world for protection and divination as well as currency (the latter in Sri Lanka and the Maldives). The style of the script suggests that this may be c. 9th-10th century. However, the angular script was often favoured for the writing of amulets and this may therefore be later. [1]

1. Porter 1998: fig. 8.5

98b.
Black limestone pebble, c. 9th–10th century
2.4 cm x 1.8cm
OA+ 13499

This amulet, with a hole though the centre, is inscribed on both sides in simple angular script with the whole of the 'throne verse' (Qur'an 2:255): *'God. There is no God but He, the Living, the Everlasting. Slumber seizes Him not neither sleep; to Him belongs all that is in the heavens and on earth. Who is there that shall intercede with Him save by His leave'* (side a). *'He knows what lies before them and what is after them, and they comprehend not anything of His knowledge save as He wills. His throne extends over the heavens and the earth; the preserving of them oppresses Him not; He is All-high, the All-glorious'* (side b).

98c.
Quartz, brown and white chalcedony, Iran, c. 18th century
3.2 cm x 4.6 cm
Sloane amulet 8

The amulet [1] is engraved with cursive inscriptions of verses from the Qur'an. In large scale in the centre is Qur'an 13:13, *'Thunder repeats his praises and so do angels with awe'*. Around the margin is the 'throne verse' (Qur'an 2: 255) (see Cat. nos. 54a-b) and one of the 'ninety-nine names' of God, *'oh Forgiver'*. This amulet belonged to Hans Sloane whose collection formed the basis of the British Museum founded in 1753.

1. Porter 1998: fig. 8.4

98d.
Quartz, white chalcedony, Iran, c. 18th century
3 cm x 4 cm
Sloane amulet 14

The amulet is engraved with cursive inscriptions in two different styles: in the centre is the word 'Muhammad SAW' referring to the Prophet. Within the word is another inscription from Qur'an 68: 51-2, *'And the unbelievers would almost trip you up with their eyes when they hear the message and they say surely he is possessed! But it is nothing less than a message to all the worlds'*. This style of script within a script, which can take elaborate forms, is sometimes known as *gulzar*. Around the margin is the 'throne verse' (Qur'an 2: 255).

98e.
Quartz, chalcedony, probably Iran, c. 19th–early 20th century, set in a silver mount with purple rope and tassels
3.5 cm x 5.2 cm (stone)
1923,0203.1

The design of the amulet is in the form of a tree with inscriptions in minute *naskh* script within the leaves, and further inscriptions in the margin. In the margin are two complete *surahs*, Qur'an: 112 and 109. The tree is made up of Qur'anic verses and benedictory phrases that are as follows:. *'Peace it is, till the rising of dawn'* (97:5); *'Thunder repeats his praises and so do angels with awe'* (13:13); *'Peace be upon the family of Elias'* (37: 130); *'Peace be upon Moses and Aaron'* (37: 120); *'Help from God and a speedy victory'* (61:13); *'Peace be upon Abraham'* (37: 109); *'Glory to God'*; *'And he who relies on God'*; *'God is great'*; *'The one who relies (on God) is for God'*; and, finally, one of 'the beautiful names of God' - *'The living'*.

98f.
Quartz, yellow chalcedony, probably Iran, c. 18th–19th century
2.8 cm x 4 cm
1867,1219.1

In minute *naskh* script, ninety-seven of 'the beautiful names of God' are inscribed. These are referred to in a number of chapters of the Qur'an as the '*asma' al-husna*' 'the beautiful names' ('There is no God but He, to Him belong the most beautiful names', Qur'an 20: 8). Among the sayings attributed to the Prophet Muhammad SAW is the statement, 'God has ninety-nine names, one hundred less one and whoever enumerates them shall enter paradise'. The *subha* (rosary) which has ninety-nine beads divided into three groups of thirty-three, is used by Muslims to meditate on the names in their prayers. Only the first few names are transcribed here: 'oh Compassionate, oh Merciful, oh King, oh Most Holy, oh Giver of Peace, oh Believer, oh Vigilant, oh Most Mighty'. The list concludes with invocations to *Imam* Hasan and *Imam* Husayn and the words 'oh *Buduh*' .This is the 3 x 3 magical square whose name itself was assigned amuletic properties.

98g.
Silver amulet c. 19th-20th century
7 cm x 8 cm
1920.81 Presented by Louis Clarke.

This is engraved on both sides with inscriptions in *naskh* script. The inscriptions, which include references to *Imam* Ali, Hasan and Husayn, indicate that this amulet was produced in a Shi'a context in Iran or elsewhere. The main text on side 'a' consists of Qur'an 2:255 and on the sides is the invocation to *Imam* Ali, ' Call upon Ali who makes wonders appear, you will find him a help to you in adversity, all care and grief will clear away through your prophethood oh Muhammad SAW through your friendship, oh Ali, oh Ali/oh Ali'. On side 'b' are the names Ali, Fatima, Hasan and Husayn, the Islamic Profession of Faith, a series of verses from the Qur'an (41:1) and the whole of *surah* 112 that lies at the heart of the Islamic faith, 'Say he is the one and only. God the eternal, absolute. He begets not nor is he begotten and there is none like unto him' (Qur'an 112).

98h.
Gold amulet, c. 18th-19th century
4 cm (diam.)
OR 0231

This amulet is inscribed in *nasta'liq* script on one side with two texts: the invocation to *Imam* Ali and Qur'an 68:51-52, 'And the unbelievers would almost trip you up with their eyes when they hear the message and they say "surely he is possessed". But it is nothing less than a message to the worlds'.

98i.
Gold amulet, c. 18th-19th century
7.1 cm x 6.4 cm
1994,0915.888 Gilbertson Bequest

On this amulet the same inscription can be found inscribed on both sides. Most interesting is the presence of the names of the 'Seven Sleepers of Ephesus' and their dog Qitmir, the only animals one of the few to enter paradise. The story of the 'Seven Sleepers' (known as the *ahl al-kahf*, the people of the cave) and their dog, which also belongs in the Christian tradition, is told in Qur'an 18:1-25. Believed to ward away evil, these names often appear on amulets. The other texts inscribed on the amulet are 'As God wills', and, in the margin, the following invocation, 'He (God) has provided safety and been kind to the one who came (the Prophet), he has been kind in what he sent down (the Qur'an), you are the strong one, deliver us from grief on the day of darkness (of judgement)'.

98j.
Carnelian amulet,
1286/1869-70
3 cm x 4.2 cm
1883,1031.21

The inscription, which consists of Qur'an 112, is acid etched to make it white. Dated amulets are relatively rare.

98k.
Red jasper seal, c.10th-11th century
1.4 cm x 1.9 cm
1880-3636 Masson collection 2

The seal [1] is engraved in reverse. This is a personal seal and used for validating documents. It is not engraved with a person's name but with a Qur'anic phrase, 'None has power over my end. God comprehends it and God is strong and able to enforce his will' (Qur'an 33: 25). This can therefore be described as an amuletic seal. Not only does it authenticate the document but the Qur'anic phrase gives protection both to the owner of the seal and to the document being sealed.

1. Porter 1998: 8.2

98l.
Nephrite amulet
2.2 cm x 4.2 cm
1893,0205.108

This is inscribed with various phrases: in the centre 'oh Judge of necessities' , around the margin the invocation to Imam Ali (Call upon Ali who makes wonders appear, you will find him a help to you in adversity, all care and grief will clear away through your friendship, oh Ali oh Ali , oh Ali) and on the sides: 'I have placed my trust in God', 'Harmony belongs to God', and two of the 'beautiful names of God', 'oh Ever Yearning' and 'oh Ever Requiting'.

98m.
Rectangular silver plaque
4.9 cm x 6.8 cm
1881,0909.11

The cursive inscription in *naskh* on eleven lines is an invocation to God in the names of two supplicants: Muhammad Ibn 'Abd Al-'Aziz (line 4) and Muhammad Ibn K-ran(?) (line 10). The first lines of the text, which starts with the *basmalah* are as follows: 'Oh God the Clement, the Indulgent, the Merciful, oh God the Abaser, Slow to anger, oh God the Living, the Everlasting oh God. Capable of all things, oh God Possessor of Glory and Generosity, oh you who Causes events to happen, oh you who Open doors, Lord of the Scriptures, open the doors of your grace to Muhammad SAW Ibn 'Abd Al-'Aziz'.

98n.
Carnelian seal engraved in reverse, c. 11th–12th century
1.5 cm x 2 cm
1866,1229.100 Duc de Blacas collection

The engraving of this seal [1] is a remarkable tour de force. In angular script are the names of the Prophet Muhammad SAW and the twelve *imams*: Ali, Hasan, Husayn, Ali, Muhammad SAW, Ja'far, Musa, Ali, Muhammad SAW, Ali, Al-Hasan, Al-Hujja. The last of the *imams*, Muhammad Al-Mahdi, also known as 'the Proof' (*Al-Hujja*) is believed to have occulted to return at some future time.

1. Reinaud 1828, ii: 196 no 85; Grohmann 1971, ii: 163 fig. 148

98o.
Carnelian set into a gold ring, c. 18th–19th century.
1.3 cm x 1.5 cm
1866,1229.99 Duc de Blacas collection

In this seal [1], the names of the twelve *imams* (the same as Cat. no. 98n except that the last *imam* is here named Muhammad SAW) make up the figure of a horseman holding a split sword in his hand. This is Ali Ibn Abi Talib (first of the Shi'a *imams*) characteristically depicted with his sword *Dhu Al-faqar* which he reputedly obtained as booty at the battle of Badr (an important event in the early history of Islam). The sword is traditionally shown as having two points and as such is believed to have magical properties. The use of calligraphy in the form of people or animals dates back to the 15th century but was particularly practised by Persian and Turkish calligraphers in the 19th century. The texts are often Shi'i in nature.

1. Reinaud 1828, ii: 193-196 no. 84

98q.
Circular silver disc, c. 20th century
3 cm (diam.)
1989,0311.1

This amulet is engraved on both sides with an interesting collection of esoteric symbols, numbers, letters and a magic square.

98p.
Octagonal silver plaque, c. 19th century
3.9 cm x 4.1 cm
1843,0609.2

The amulet is inscribed in cursive script on both sides. In the centre of side 'a', the Islamic Profession of Faith (*Shahadah*) with, around the margin, two verses, Qur'an 12: 64 and 61:13. The latter is known as the 'victory verse' and states, 'Help from God and a speedy victory so give the glad tidings to the believers'. On the other side, following the *Basmalah*, are groups of the 'mysterious letters of the Qur'an'.

98s.
Magical brass arm amulet, probably Iran, c. 19th century
7.5 cm x 9.7 cm (irreg.)
1891,0418.42

Arm amulets engraved with magic squares and Qur'anic verses were worn to give protection. In the centre of this example is a lion whose body is made up of a 4 x 4 magical square. Undeciphered words make up the inside of his head and rear. A sun with the upper part of a face is behind the lion. The motif of lion and sun has a long history in the Near East, being principally a zodiacal symbol associated with Leo. In 19th century Iran, it became the national symbol of the Qajars, where the lion often brandishes the split sword of Ali.

98u.
Nephrite amulet, possibly India, c. 18th–19th century
4.5 cm x 4.8 cm
1867,0709.7

This amulet, which was intended to be worn, is inscribed with a series of lines of letters and numbers and magical words. What they actually signify remains a mystery. There is in Islam a vast literature known as 'the science of the letters' which consists of studies on particular properties of letters. Within this there are for example letters of darkness or brotherly love, and letters of fire such as *alif, ha* and *ta* which ward off evils associated with cold.

98t.
Brass magical seal, c. 19th century
2.8 cm (diam.), 3.5 cm (length, including handle)
1893,0205.101

The names of angels often appear on amulets inscribed around the sides of magic squares as in this example. The four archangels, known as 'the sultans of angels' are each believed to be endowed with special gifts and functions: Jibra'il (Gabriel), the messenger to the Prophets through whom the Qur'an was transmitted; Mika'il, who presides over rain and plants; Israfil, who stands beside the throne guarding the heavenly trumpet; and Uzrafil, the angel of death. The magic square here is made up of the 'mysterious letters' *kaf ha ya ayn* and *sad* from the beginning of *Surah* 19.

98r.
Brass magical amulet used for healing, c. 19th century
7 cm (diam.)
1893,0215.1

This is an amulet [1] used for stamping onto paper in the case of illness. It is engraved on both sides – its handle can be unscrewed and attached to the other side. On one side it includes six passages from the Qur'an which contain the verb for healing *sh f y* and the 3 x 3 square known as *buduh* (after the letters *ba', dal, waw,* and *ha,* which are in the four corners of the square) that itself is associated with healing. [2] Around the square are the four archangels: Jibra'il, Mika'il, Israfil and Uzrail. On the other side there are other verses from the Qur'an, more magic squares and some of 'the mysterious letters of the Qur'an'. Magical squares are regarded as one of the most impressive achievements of Muslim mathematicians. The link between making squares and magic began with the representation of religious phrases or 'the names of God' numerically according to the old order of the Semitic alphabet known as *abjad*. In this system, *alif* = 1, *ba* = 2, *jim* = 3 and so on. Magic squares of any size could be created and in all cases it is intended that the numbers should be equal in whichever direction they are added together. In the case of the 3 x 3 square the numbers all add up to 15.

1. Porter 1998: 8.6
2. Maddison and Savage-Smith 1997:59 ff.

4	9	2
3	5	7
8	1	6

99a.

99c.

99e.

99f.

99a-g.
A group of Islamic style magic coins from the Malay Peninsula, 1950s and later.
3.6 cm to 3.9 cm (diam.)
1980,0303.1; 1998,0105.6; 1992,1043.1; 1995,0857.3; 1980,0105.8; 1998,0105.2;
1998,0105.3

The designs on these amulets [1] (decorated on both sides), which are in the form of European style coins, represent images of Prophets referred to in the Qur'an, as well as historical figures, animals and landscapes. They are frequently accompanied by Arabic texts that name the images or invoke God's protection. 'A' has an image of Khidr, the Prophet-saint, the guide to travellers, and on the back the names of the four 'rightly guided caliphs' – Abu Bakr, Umar, Uthman and Ali – with the additional word *Yasin* (two of the 'mysterious letters' often treated as a single word). 'B' has an old man surrounded by figures depicted in shadow-puppet style with, above, the Islamic Profession of Faith. On the back is a building that possibly represents the Ka'ba at Mecca. 'C' has a bird on one side and Arabic inscriptions on the other that include the words, Allah, Muhammad SAW and some of the 'mysterious letters of the Qur'an'. 'D' has an old man with a stick who is named as Isa (Jesus), with the word *Yasin* in an attractive design on the back. 'E' has a man in Arab head-dress named Ali holding a sword. This is Ali Ibn Abi Talib, one of the 'rightly guided caliphs' and the first of the Shi'i *imams*, a building on his back. 'F' has two old men facing each other, one of whom is named Isa. On the back, the inscriptions include the 'four caliphs'. 'G' has two old men facing each other, named as Ayyub (Job) and Idris. The back includes two *kris* with crossed swords pointing upwards with puppet-head handles, and again the names of the 'four caliphs'.

1. Cribb 1999: nos. 262, 268, 277,332, 303,304,308

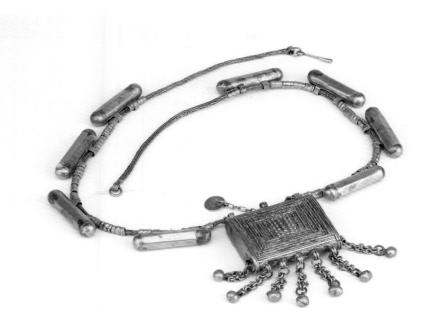

100.
Silver necklace with amulet holder, Yemen, 19th-20th century, and two paper amulets
Necklace
45 cm (length)
1999,0413.1

Paper charms
33 cm (length) 10 cm (width); 103 cm (length) 5 cm (width)
1999,0413.8; 1999,0413.13
Acquired in Yemen and presented by Michael Macdonald

The style of the necklace is typical of the silver jewellery of Yemen, much of which was traditionally made by Jewish craftsmen. Inside the amulet holder were found a number of paper charms, two of which are included here. These are inscribed with verses from the Qur'an, groups of *'the mysterious letters of the Qur'an'*, magical squares and 'the seven magical signs'. These protective signs (found on the paper amulet to the right of the magical square) denote the most important of *'the beautiful names of God'* and sometimes appear on their own on amulets.
VP

101.
Cast brass talismanic plaque
11.5 cm x 9cm
OA+ 2606

The plaque is decorated on both sides. The scene illustrated represents at the top, Solomon, who features in the Qur'an as lord of the winds, the *jinns* (genies), and who can talk to animals and birds. He is surrounded by his *jinns* and around the edge are magical signs and strange symbols that resemble ancient scripts. Mysterious and indecipherable, these scripts were considered magical.
VP

102.
Stone amulet mould,
probably Obsidian, acquired
in Iraq
6 cm (length), 5.8 cm
(width)
1921,0511.1

This is part of a mould that would have been used to make a cylindrical amulet with the lost wax casting method. From the wax, a clay core would have been made from which the metal amulet would have been produced. The runnels at the top were used to pour in the wax and the pieces of the mould were held in place with pegs. The durability of the material ensured that despite its fine decoration it could frequently have been re-used. The designs consist of the repetition of the words, *'ya (oh) Ali'*, and scratched across the top are the words *'oh Ali, through God'*. Moulds such as this are rare and this item is comparable to a mould in the Ashmolean Museum acquired in Syria. [1]

1. Spink 1986: 9
VP

103.
Tinned copper footed bowl,
(*jam*) made in western
Iran, dated in numerals
1070/1659
36 cm (diam.)
1984,0128.1

The main design is the inscription written in elegant *nasta'liq* which lies against a floral ground. In Arabic it calls God's blessings upon the *'Fourteen Protected Ones'* (the twelve *imams* and the Prophet Muhammad SAW and his daughter Fatima). They are given in the form of their name and attribute. For example, 'Ali the chosen one', 'Hasan the pleasing', 'Husayn the martyr'. [1] It is interesting to note that Arabic still continued as the preferred language for religious inscriptions while Persian was read and spoken by the majority of the population at this time.

1. A similar footed bowl dated 1017/1608-9 is published in Melikian-Chirvani 1982: 328
VP

104a
Steel sword inlaid with gold, mid 19th century Iran.
1878,1230.824
L.96cm

At the top of the blade is the name of the Qajar ruler Muhammad Shah (1834-48). It was the custom for rulers to hand out swords as gifts. Muhammad Shah was known for his austere character and mystical leanings. This may in part explain the motif on the one side which consists of a double-headed axe, a symbol with Sufi associations. The blade and the hilt are covered with a number of protective inscriptions. On both sides of the blade are a number of the ninety-nine names of God while on the blunt side of the blade are the names of the seven sleepers of Ephesus.
VP

104.
Writing board, West Africa, c. 19th century or earlier
32 cm (height)
Private collection

Children, particularly in Africa, learnt to read and write the Qur'an using writing boards known as *lawh*. They would start with the short *surahs* and gradually working their way through to the longer ones. When a child had memorised a chapter, water was used to wipe the board clean. It was essential however that the water was preserved. This water was believed to contain the words of God was regarded as efficacious against numerous afflictions. The inscription in a form of *maghribi* script is inscribed on one side (illustrated) with *Surah* 106 ('Quraysh'). Both show traces of where a previous *surah* has been wiped off, *Surah* 107 ('Ma'un').[1]

1. For other examples see Bravman 1983: 61
VP

105
Standard, copper, in the form of a hand,
probably Iran c.18th-19th century.
1863 11-1
H.41cm

This standard is in the form of a hand. In some areas it is known as 'the hand of Fatima', the daughter of the Prophet Muhammad SAW, the source of numerous legends who has a huge following among Sunnis and Shi'a. In Iran, although Fatima is widely revered among the Shi'a, the hand is known as the 'hand of Abbas', Husayn's half-brother and standard-bearer who lost both arms in the battle of Kerbela; yet fought on'. The hand is engraved on both sides. On one side are the names of the Shi'i imams, on the other are confronting winged horses standing on either side of a domed building, presumably The Dome of the Rock in Jerusalem. The winged horse is known as Buraq and is the horse upon which the Prophet Muhammad SAW rode on his night journey to heaven.
VP

105a.
Standard (*alam*), gilded
brass, Iran, 17th century
128 cm (height)
1888,0901.17

Alams were carried in religious processions, particularly at the annual *Muharram* (the first month of the Muslim year) ceremony which commemorates the martyrdom of the Shi'i *Imam* Husayn, grandson of the Prophet Muhammad SAW, at the battle of Kerbela in 680. This tragic event features strongly in the religious life of the Shi'i sect of Islam. In its shape, the standard also symbolises the sword of *Imam* Ali. The inscriptions are in open-work against an elaborate floral background. The words God, Muhammad SAW, Fatima, Hasan and Husayn are set in a beautiful composition in bold script with the invocation '*Oh Ali*' in a roundel above. Along the '*blade*' of the *alam* the names are repeated in open-work cartouches. This is one of a pair. [1]

1. Canby 1999: 169
VP

106a.

106a-b.
Two Amulet pendants
The Malay world
20th century
1998.1.4294 &
1998.1.4295

The following pendants were made for the local communities to seek protection from Allah and attest to their utmost dependency on Him. They are made of brass in the shape of coins. Pendant (a) reveals the name of Allah alternating a six sided star. It was enameled in red, a popular colour in the Southeast. Asia and China. The outer shape of the pendant is a multi petalled flower adorned with raised string work in the shape of scrolls and loops.

Pendant (b) displays in its centre a six sided star with the word Allah occupying its corners. Surrounding the central roundel is a ring of vegetal decoration which is pierced, and at the rim are three loops where it would have been hanged.

Pendants in the form of amulets were popular accessories in Asia.
HB

106b.

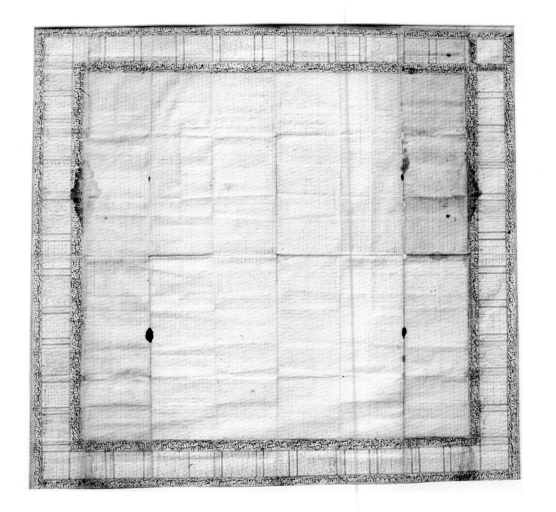

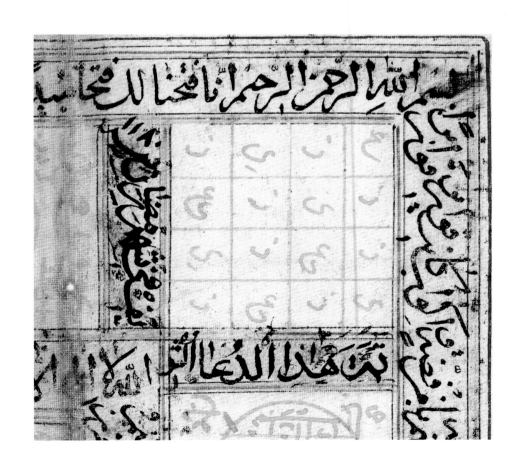

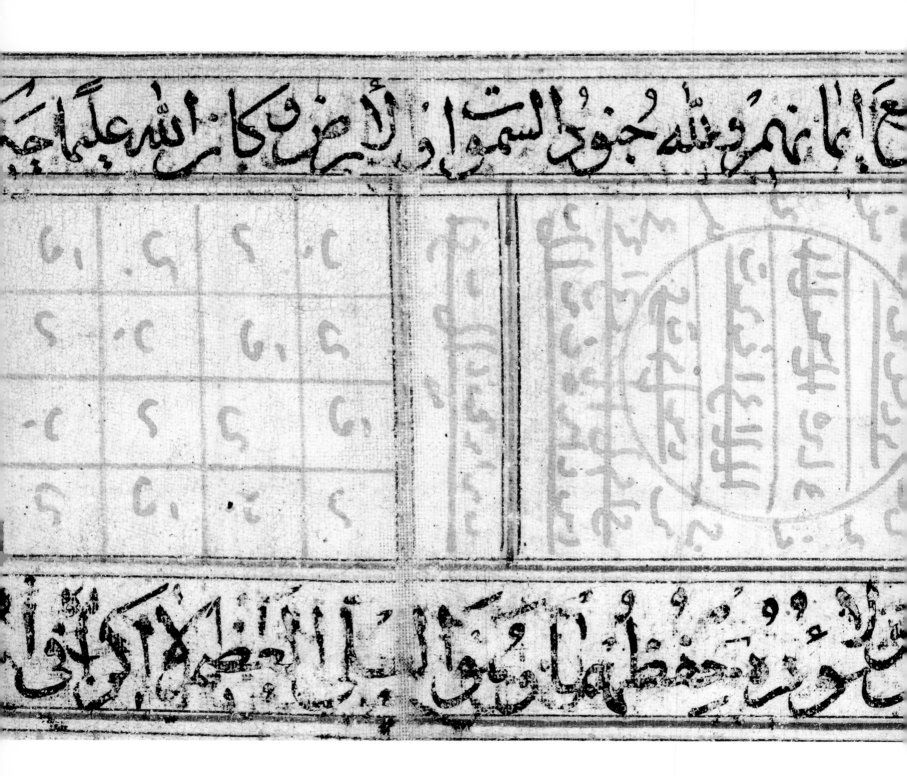

وَللَّهِ جُنُودُ السَّمَوَاتِ وَالْأَرْضِ وَكَانَ اللَّهُ عَلِيمًا حَكِيمًا

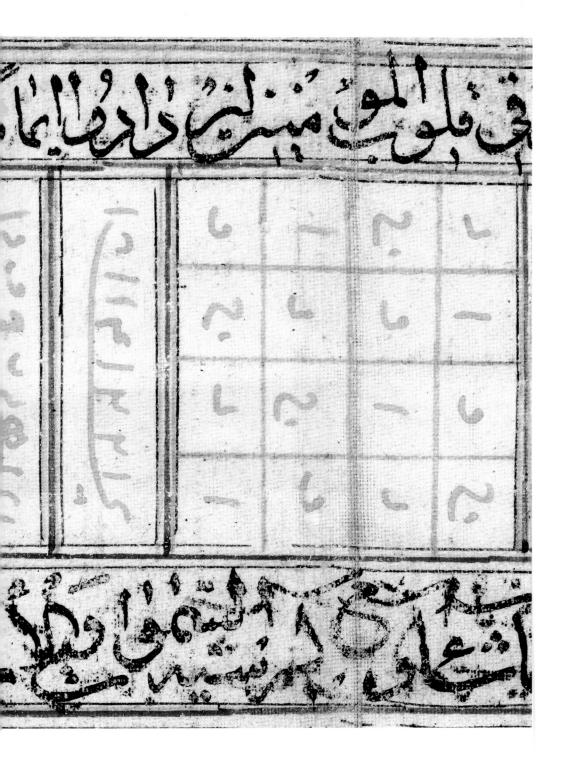

107.
Talismanic chart on fabric
Iran
1180 H/1766 AD
70 cm x 70 cm
2001.1.86

The talismanic chart is divided into a border and field by two narrow bands of black *naskh* script that recall the Qur'anic *Surahs of Al Fath* (the Victory), *Al Balad* (The City) and *Al Nas* (Man). The inner border contains *Ayat Al Kursi* (The Throne Verses) ; *Surah Al Baqarah* (The Cow; verse 255), and frames the field which comprises a massive chart of 100 x 100 squares of single Arabic letters in gold. The extensive use of magic squares numbering up to 10,000 individual cells, is a characteristic of the Qajar period. The chart is referred to as a plea or prayer and is dated to Ramadan 1180 H/ 1766 AD. The border of the chart comprises 4 x 4 squares employing names and attributes to Allah that are formed in four letters. Among the names are Al Aziz (the mighty), Al Jamil (the beautiful), and Al Hasib (the reckoner). Talismanic charts that were folded were regarded as personal amulets, carried by their commissioner for protection from misfortunes.
HB

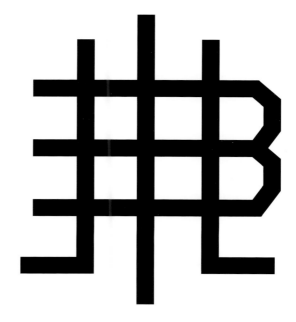

108.
Lobmeyr Glass
Turkey
1914-1916 AD/1330-1332
H
Height 10.8 cm
2003.10.36

Lobmeyr flourished during the 19th and 20th centuries. Its founder was Josef Lobmeyr (1792-1855) a designer and commissioner of glass ware. He opened a store in 1823 selling the commissioned glass. By the mid 19th century, the store ordered enamel Bohemian painted glass from Anton Egermann. And during the early 20th century they worked with of Meyer's Neffe and Kralik. The art director during the early 20th century was Josef Hoffman and the commissioned artists were Michael Powolny, and Adolf Loos.

The Lobmeyr glass is part of a set commissioned by the Ottoman elite. The glass is hand blown, cut, engraved and enameled. Polished by hand, the glass reveals the beauty of the Arabic script through its balanced shape. The glass is divided into three rings each including a calligraphic band. The date 1914-16 is indicated in AD and *Hijri* dates, indicating that the commissioner sent the exact message to be copied on the glass.

The Lobmeyr glass mark adds to the importance of the beaker.
HB

The Contemporary
Art of Writing and Calligraphy

The shapes of the Arabic letter forms continue to inspire artists today. Included here is the work of various artists. Some are calligraphers trained in the traditional manner, while others use script or pseudo-script in different and innovative ways.

Arabic calligraphy portrayed an identity that the contemporary calligrapher expressed proudly. Contemporary calligraphers from Malaysia supplemented the calligraphy with a decorative repertoire indigenous to the Malay region.

They composed their calligraphic folios from popular verses and Hadith, and retained a simple composition, aiming to make the meaning of the words of God easily decipherable. The meaning and respect for the religious text, guides the calligrapher and limits the development of the decorative repertoire.

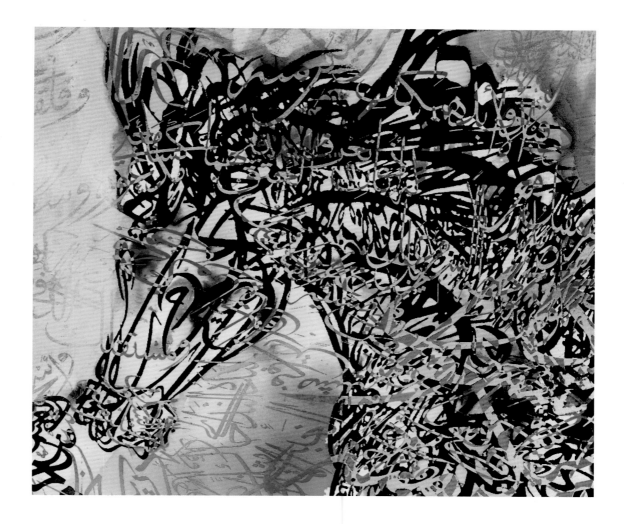

109.
Ahmed Moustafa,
Frolicking horses, **Iris**
print, edition of 3, 1993
52 cm x 40 cm
Courtesy the artist

This extraordinary calligraphic composition [1] is inspired by the poetry of the pre-Islamic poet Imru'l Qais in praise of the Arab horse:

'Often have I been off with the morn, the birds yet asleep in their nests, my horse short-haired, outstripping the wild game, huge-bodied, charging, fleet-fleeting, head-foremost, head-long, all together. The match of a rugged boulder hurled from on high by the torrent. A chestnut-horse, sliding the saddle-felt from his back, just as a smooth pebble slides off the rain cascading. Fiery he is, for all his leanness, and when his ardour boils on him he roars...'

The use of calligraphy to create images is a tradition well known in Turkey and Iran. Moustafa has re-invented the form and exploited its dramatic possibilities to the full. Ahmed Moustafa was born in Egypt and has lived in London since the 1970s. He graduated from the Faculty of Fine Arts, University of Alexandria, where he was appointed lecturer. He carried out his postgraduate studies at Central St Martins College of Art, London, where he was granted his Ph.D in 1989 on the scientific foundation of Arabic letter-shapes. His work combines a deep historical knowledge of the Arabic classical tradition as well as an enormous power for innovation and he is represented in numerous public and private collections.

1. Henzell-Thomas 1998
2. I am grateful to Ahmed Moustafa for the translation
VP

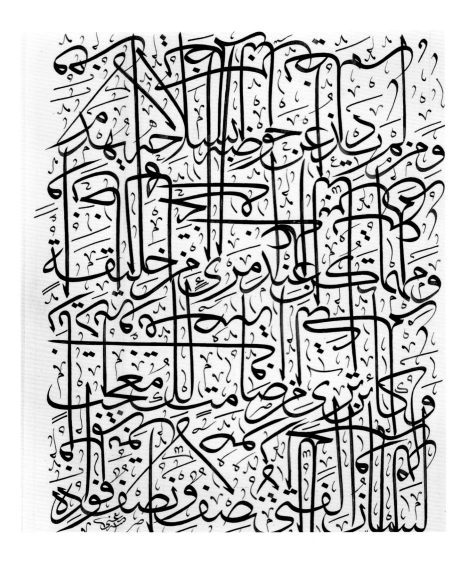

110.
Ghani Alani, From the
Mu'allaqat **of** ***Zoheir***, **ink**
on paper, c.1990s
60 cm x 50 cm
2003,0228.03 (0328)

Inscribed in *muhaqqaq* script and written in different directions are verses by the pre-Islamic poet Zoheir (530-627) which begin:

Whoever does not oppress others is oppressed himself, whoever persists in his obstinacy from afar finishes by mistaking the enemy for a friend, and he who does not respect himself shall not be respected. Whatever a man's nature he had better believe himself capable of hiding it ...'[1]

Alani was born in Baghdad but has been living in Paris since the 1960s. He obtained his *ijaza* from two masters, Hashem Al-Khattat Al-Baghdadi and the Turkish master Hamid Al-Amidi. He teaches, publishes and exhibits his work extensively.[2]

1. I am grateful to Ghani Alani for the translation.
2. See for example Guesdon et. al 2001: 179; Alani 2001
VP

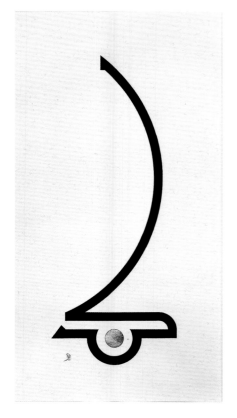

111.
Nassar Mansour, ***Kun***, **ink**
and gold on paper, 2003
H.46 cm x W.25 cm
Courtesy of the artist

Jordanian calligrapher Mansour recently obtained his *ijaza* from the renowned Turkish calligrapher Ustadh Hasan Celebi. He lives in London and studies at the Visual Islamic and Traditional Arts Institute. He has undertaken a number of architectural calligraphic commissions for monuments in Jordan and has recently published a book on the *ijaza*.[1] In this composition the word *kun* (Be) is simply inscribed in *kufic* script. The word alludes

to the phrase in the Qur'an, 'and the day he (God) says "Be", and it is' (Qur'an 2:117)

1. Mansour 2000
VP

112.
The Late Tahirruddin bin Jamaludin
1st Prize winner, Manifestasi Perdana Seni Khat (calligraphy competition), Kuala Lumpur, 1999

Tahirruddin bin Jamaludin was an inspiring Malaysian artist creating outstanding compositions with the words of a popular Arabic saying: *"the promise of the generous is a debt."* The artist endeavoured to represent his identity as a Muslim through the Arabic letters and as a Malaysian through the use of batik as a background. Batik colours and patterns are a traditional Southeast Asian craft. Batik, also known, as the resist method, is a process involving the waxing of a textile surface, dyeing the material, re-waxing and re-dyeing to create an intricate pattern and design. The beauty of this pattern stems from its natural flow, and the vertical alignment complements the calligraphic foreground. The inscribed letters are interwoven within each other, blending in a manner that presents the three words as a unit. The calligraphy protrudes in a three dimensional composition and the signature of the artist is at the bottom of the text box, stressing the importance of calligraphy and his satisfaction with the composition. Tahirruddin bin Jamaludin worked at Edusystem Sdn Bhd as a designer, a time during which he learned Arabic calligraphy under Ustaz Mohammed Yusof Abu Bakar, President of the National Association of Islamic Calligraphy, Malaysia.
HB

113.
Zainurrahman Afandi
1st Prize winner
Manifestasi Perdana Seni Khat (calligraphy competition),
Kuala Lumpur, 2001

Zainurrahman is a professional calligrapher, a member of the National Association of Islamic Calligraphy Malaysia and a student of Ustaz Mohammad Yusof Abu Bakar. Part of his fame comes from inscribing the full Qur'an Mushaf in beautiful calligraphy.

The panel exhibits the words of *Surah Al Rahman* (55:24) *"and his are the ships sailing smoothly through the seas, lofty as mountains."* As the verse refers to seas, the calligrapher creates a blue background that is full of energy and mystery. The Arabic calligraphy intermingles within the waves of the background leading to vibrant movement within the composition. Yet the harmonious colours of the composition sets the viewer in an inspiring atmosphere.
HB

114.
Mohd Effy Saiful bin Mohd Fathil
1st Prize winner
Manifestasi Perdana Seni Khat (calligraphy competition),
Kuala Lumpur, 2003

In a well balanced yet traditional composition, inscribed in white against a plain purple background the words of the *Surah Al Zariyat* (51:20-21): *"On the earth are signs for those of assured faith, and also in your own selves: will ye not then see?"* The Malaysian artist combined different styles of traditional calligraphy and created a well flowing rhythmic composition. He felt the need to confine the words into rectangular units and accordingly made use of sporadic small dots to fill the space in between. The concept of "horror vacuum" was tackled by medieval Islamic artists and calligraphers, throughout the Islamic periods, in different manners. Spiral pattern and arabesque scrolls were two of the main motifs that occupied backgrounds.
HB

Composed of tiny drops in a plentitude of colours, the Malaysian artist Abd Shukor bin Yahya created a wonderful and serene composition of a phrase from the Islamic tradition: *"Those who seek The Might, it's God that totally encompasses The Might."* The artist successfully created out of sporadic droplets an outstanding composed space, philosophically leading the mind to focus on the origin of everything, in the spirit of a monotheistic approach. The calligraphy is rendered in a lighter pigment in a three dimensional manner, making the words easy to read and understand, hence, the artist has combined beauty, philosophy and meaning. Abd Shukor bin Yahya was a participant of Manifestasi Perdana Seni Khat, Kuala Lumpur, an annual calligraphy competition of Malaysia and was recognized for his innovation and creativity.
HB

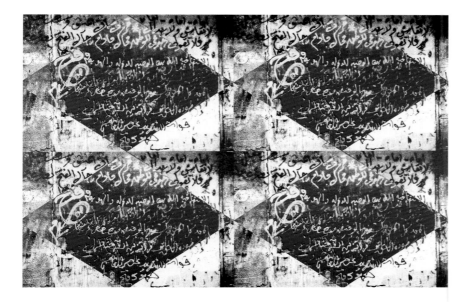

116
'Letter to a Mother' by Palestinian artist Laila Shawa,
Lithograph 45/50 1992.
1994,0726.02
H. 38cm x W.58cm
Shawa and Wijdan 1994

This work is part of a series called 'The walls of Gaza' inspired by the grafitti written in Gaza during the first Palestinian uprising. Shawa describes the writing as a 'spontaneous form of calligraphy' which has also been described by Wijdan Ali as 'calligrafiti' (see Cat.No 48). Her intention was to convey the ephemeral and changing messages written with spray paint. Purple was the colour used by the Israeli army to paint over grafitti. Laila Shawa was born in Gaza and studied art in Egypt and Italy and with the Austrian expressionist Oskar Kokoschka. She has exhibited widely and her work is in a number of public and private collections. She has lived in London since 1987.
VP

The Islamic World After 1500 AD

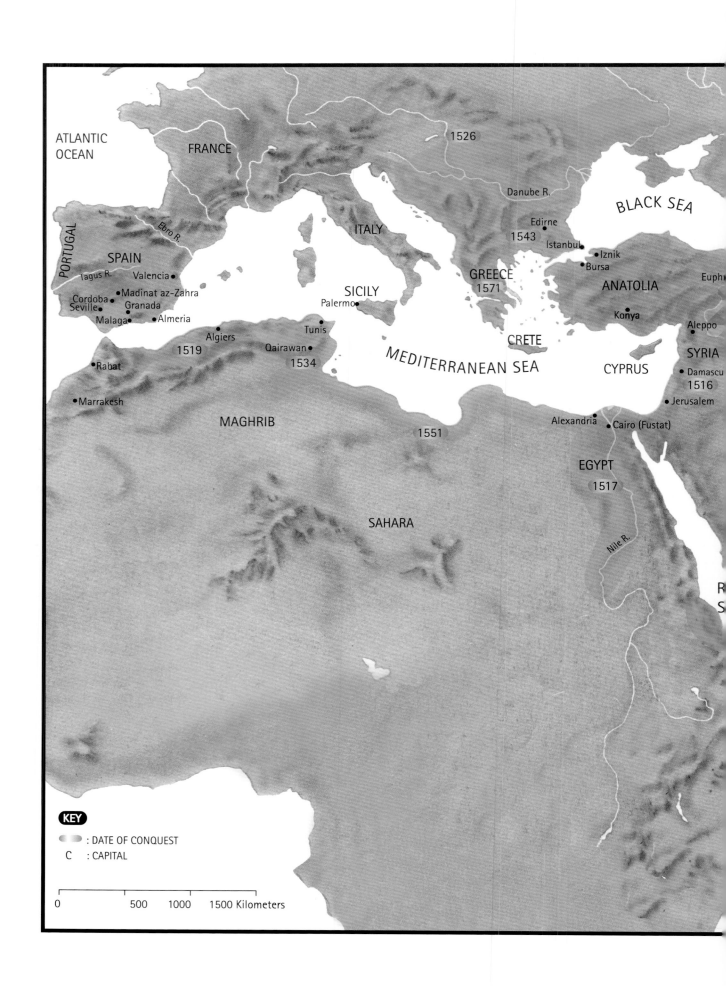

ATLANTIC OCEAN

FRANCE

1526

Danube R.

BLACK SEA

PORTUGAL

Ebro R.

ITALY

Edirne

1543

Istanbul

Iznik

Bursa

GREECE

1571

ANATOLIA

Euphr

SPAIN

Tagus R.

Valencia

Madinat az-Zahra

Cordoba

Granada

Seville

Malaga

Almeria

SICILY

Palermo

Konya

Aleppo

Algiers

1519

Tunis

Qairawan

1534

CRETE

MEDITERRANEAN SEA

CYPRUS

SYRIA

Damascu

1516

Rabat

Jerusalem

Marrakesh

MAGHRIB

1551

Alexandria

Cairo (Fustat)

EGYPT

1517

SAHARA

Nile R.

R
S

KEY

: DATE OF CONQUEST

C : CAPITAL

0   500   1000   1500 Kilometers

222

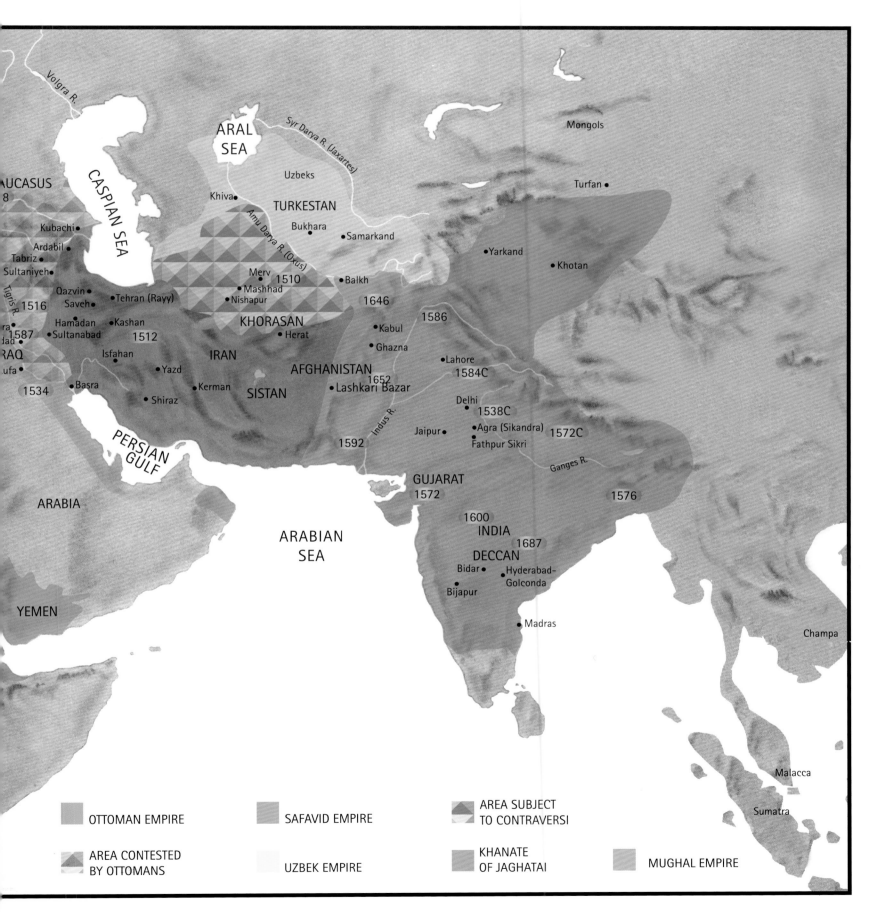

ARAL
SEA

Volgra R.

CASPIAN SEA

Syr Darya R. (Jaxartes)

Mongols

Uzbeks

Khiva •

TURKESTAN

Bukhara •

Samarkand •

Turfan •

UCASUS
8

Kubachi •

Ardabil •

Tabriz •

Sultaniyeh •

Amu Darya R. (Oxus)

Merv •   1510

Balkh •

Yarkand •

Khotan •

Mashhad •

Tigris R.

1516

Qazvin •   Saveh •   • Tehran (Rayy)

Nishapur •

1646

1586

• Kabul

Hamadan •   • Kashan

KHORASAN

ra

1587   • Sultanabad   1512

• Herat

• Ghazna

ad

Isfahan •

IRAN

AFGHANISTAN

• Lahore

1584C

ufa

• Yazd

• Kerman

SISTAN

1652
• Lashkari Bazar

Delhi
•   1538C

• Basra

1534

• Shiraz

1592

Jaipur •

• Agra (Sikandra)
• Fathpur Sikri

1572C

PERSIAN
GULF

Indus R.

Ganges R.

GUJARAT
1572

1576

ARABIA

ARABIAN
SEA

1600

INDIA

1687

Bidar •

Champa

DECCAN

Hyderabad–
Golconda

YEMEN

• Bijapur

• Madras

Malacca

Sumatra

OTTOMAN EMPIRE

SAFAVID EMPIRE

AREA SUBJECT
TO CONTRAVERSI

AREA CONTESTED
BY OTTOMANS

UZBEK EMPIRE

KHANATE
OF JAGHATAI

MUGHAL EMPIRE

Table of Scripts

'Nun. By the pen and what they inscribe.'
Qur'an *Surah* 68:1

'The Pen' copied in different scripts by Nassar Mansour

Kufic – was a script whose development from the end of the 7th century has been associated with the city of Kufa in Iraq. It is characterised by angular letter forms and was widely used until about the 12th century. It was the principal script in the early period for copying Qur'ans. The simple and elegant forms were embellished over time.

Eastern *kufic* – was developed by Persian calligraphers during the 10th century and is distinguished by short, sharply angled strokes. This led to its description as 'bent *kufic*' by Western scholars.

Maghribi kufic – developed in North Africa (the Maghreb) and Spain in the 10th century and is characterized by a rounding of the angles of *kufic* script. Forms of this script are still used in the region to this day.

Naskh – the cursive copyist's hand predominantly used from the 12th century for writing government documents in addition to copying the Qur'an. It is one of the 'six calligraphic styles' refined by the calligrapher Ibn Muqla.

Thuluth – meaning one third and one of Ibn Muqla's 'six calligraphic styles' is a large scale cursive script often used for monumental inscriptions and particularly favoured by the Mamluk rulers of Egypt (1250-1517).

Nasta`liq – the 'hanging' script, described as 'the bride of the Islamic styles of writing' was reputedly developed in the 13th century but legend has it that it was perfected by the calligrapher Mir Ali of Tabriz (d.1446) after dreaming of flying geese. It appears predominantly in Iran and India from about the 16th century.

Divani – was a highly elaborate script developed by Ottoman Turkish calligraphers during the 15th century. It was particulalry used for chancellery documents such as firmans.

Square kufic – was developed in the 13th century for ornamental use after regular *kufic* has been superseded. As shown here, it frequently appears in a square on coins of the Mongols and their successors on architecture and elsewhere.

The Six Calligraphic Styles (*al-aqlam al-sitta*)

By the 10th century, there were said to be at least twenty different cursive styles of script which had proliferated over the years, largely used for personal correspondence or to meet the needs of the bureaucrats and merchants. This was in contrast to the *kufic* script used to copy the Qur'an. Charged with the task of standardising and refining the myriad cursive scripts, was the great calligrapher Muhammad Ibn Muqla (d.940) a vizier at the court of three Abbasid Caliphs. He and later Ibn Bawwab (d.1022) established what are known as the 'six calligraphic styles' *al- aqlam al-sitta*. The aim was to formalize a system for the writing of cursive scripts which would make them as well proportioned and as beautiful as the *kufic* script and therefore appropriate for writing the Qur'an.

Thuluth

ن وَٱلْقَلَمِ وَمَا يَسْطُرُونَ

Naskh

ن وَٱلْقَلَمِ وَمَا يَسْطُرُونَ

Muhaqqaq

ن وَٱلْقَلَمِ وَمَا يَسْطُرُونَ

Raihan

ن وَٱلْقَلَمِ وَمَا يَسْطُرُونَ

Tawqi`

ن وَٱلْقَلَمِ وَمَا يَسْطُرُونَ

Riqa`

ن وَٱلْقَلَمِ وَمَا يَسْطُرُونَ

The System of Proportion of the Arabic letter forms developed by Ibn Muqla

The guiding principle was the use of a circle, the letter *alif* and a 'rhombic' dot. The 'rhombic' dot is formed by pressing the pen diagonally on paper so that the length of the dot's equal sides are the same as the width of the pen. The *alif* is a vertical stroke measuring a specific number of 'rhombic' dots. The circle has a diameter equal to the leghth of the *alif* and provides the proportional grid for all the letters. The various cursive styles are ultimately based on the width of the pens chosen by the scribe and the number of dots used to fashion the *alif*; these can be five to seven in number. The advantage of the system was that it meant that the calligrapher could work in larger or smaller formats simply by varying the size of the nib; the letters would always be in proportion to each other.

The letter *alif* (a) made up of seven rhombic dots

The letter *ra'* (r)

The letter *dal* (d)

The letter *nun* (n)

The letter *ha'* (hard h)

The *Tughra* of Sultan Suleyman the Magnificent (1520-66)

The *tughra* was the intricate device that served as the imperial monograms of the Ottoman sultans of Turkey. First adopted on documents and coins from the 14th century, each sultan generally chose the precise form of his *tughra* on the day of his accession from specimens prepared for him in advance.

The *tughra* is made up of the words: 'Suleyman Shah Ibn Selim Shah Khan Al-Muzaffar *daima'* (Suleyman Shah son of Selim Shah Khan the ever victorious). Each section has its own particular name: the cluster of letters at the base which make up his name is called the 'palm of the hand' or ' the pedestal'. The two large loops on the left which are exagerated forms of the letter *nun* (n) are known as the inner and outer eggs. These are intersected by the uprights of the word *muzaffar* (victorious). Within the inner loop is the word *daima* (ever). The three uprights are known as banners.

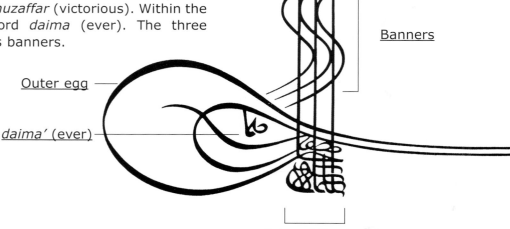

Banners

Outer egg

daima' (ever)

Palm of the hand
Muzaffar (victorious)
Suleyman Shah Ibn Selim Shah Khan

Bibliography and further reading

Adamova, A.T., 'On the attribution of Persian painting and drawings to the time of Shah 'Abbas I', in R Hillenbrand (ed.), *Persian painting from the Mongols to the Qajars*: studies in honour of Basil W Robinson, IB Taurus, London, 2000.

Achjadi, Judi, *Batik: Spirit of Indonesia*, Yayasan Batik Indonesia, West Java, 1999.

Afshar, I., *Historical Monuments of Yazd and Archaeological Remains,* 2 vols. Tehran 1354/1976.

Ak Akce, *Mongol and Ilkhanid Coins,* Yapi Credi Coin Collection-I, 1992.

Alani, G., *Calligraphie Arabe,* Editions Fleurus, Paris, 2001.

——& JC Meffre, *Une geste des signes*, Fata Morgana, Paris, 2002.

Album, S., *A checklist of Islamic coins,* Stephen Album, Santa Rosa, 1998.

Al-Faruqi, Ismail, *The Cultural Atlas of Islam,* Macmillan, Publishing Company, New York, 1986.

Al-Jaber, Ibrahim Jaber, *Arab Islamic Coins,* vol.2, Al-Ahleia Press, Qatar, 1992.

Ali, Abdullah Yusuf. *The Holy Quran – text and translation,* Islamic Book Trust, Kuala Lumpur, 1994.

Ali, Zakaria, Islamic Art in Southeast Asia- 830 AD- 1570AD, Dewan Bahasa dan Pustaka, 1994.

Al Maqrizi,Taqi al Din Ahmad, *Al-mawa'iz waal'itibar fi dhikr al- Khitat,* 2 Vol, Cairo: Bulaq Press Edition, 1853.

Arberry, A.J., *The Koran interpreted,* 2 vols, Allen & Unwin, London, 1955.

The arts of Islam, Hayward Gallery, London, 1976.

As-Suyuti, Jalalu'd-Din Abd'ur-Rahman As-Suyuti, *Medicine of the Prophet* (pbuh), Ta-Ha Publisher Ltd., London, 1999.

Atasoy, N. & J. Raby, *Iznik: the pottery of Ottoman Turkey,* Alexandria Press in assoc. with Thames & Hudson, London, 1989.

Atil, Esin. *Age of Sultan Suleyman the Magnificent,* National Gallery of Art, Washington, 1987.

—— (ed.), *Islamic Art & Patronage,* The al-Sabah Collection, New York, 1990.

—— *Art of the Mamluks*, Washington 1981.

Auld, S., 'Kuficising inscriptions in the work of Gentile da Fabriano', *Oriental Art,* vol. 32, no. 3, 1986, pp. 246–66.

Badger, George Percy, *An English – Arabic Lexicon,* Librairie Du Liban, Beirut, 1980-1988.

Baer, E., *Metalwork in medieval Islamic art,* State University of New York Press, Albany, 1983.

Barrett, D., *Islamic metalwork in the British Museum,* British Museum Press, London, 1949.

Bayani, M., *Ahval va athar-i khvush-nivisan,* Danishgah-i Tihran, Tehran, 1966–69.

Bayani, Manjeh, Anna Contadini, Tim Stanley, The Nasser D. Khalili Collection of Islamic Art - *The Decorated Word,* The Nour Foundation, England, 1996.

Begley, W.E., *Monumental Islamic calligraphy from India,* Islamic Foundation, Illinois, 1985.

"Bihar", *Encyclopaedia of Islam,* new edn, vol. I, Brill, Leiden, 1978, pp. 1209.

Blair, S., 'The coins of the later Ilkhanids' *Journal of the Economic and Social History of the Orient* 26 (October 1983) 295-317.

Blair, S., 'What is the date of the Dome of the Rock?' in Raby, J. and J. Johns (eds) *Bayt al-Maqdis:'Abd al-Malik's Jerusalem, Part one,* Oxford Studies in Islamic Art , Oxford, 59-88

Blair, S., *Islamic inscriptions,* Edinburgh University Press, 1998.

——& J Bloom, *The art and architecture of Islam 1250 – 1800,* Yale University Press, New Haven & London, 1995.

——& J Bloom, *Islamic arts,* Phaidon, London, 1997.

Bloom, J., *Paper before print. The history and impact of paper in the Islamic world,* Yale University Press, New Haven & London, 2001.

Bosworth, C.E., *The new Islamic dynasties,* Edinburgh University Press, 1996.

Bravmaan, R. ,*African Islam,* Smithsonian Institutution Press, Washington D.C. 1983

Brend, B., *Islamic art,* British Museum Press, London, 1991.

Broome, M., *A handbook of Islamic coins,* Seaby, London, 1985.

Caiger-Smith, A., *Lustre pottery: technique, tradition and innovation in Islam,* Faber and Faber, London, 1985.

Canaan, T., 'The decipherment of Arabic talismans, part 1', *Berytus: Archaeological Studies,* vol. 4, 1937, pp. 69–110.

——'The decipherment of Arabic talismans, part 2', *Berytus: Archaeological Studies,* vol. 5, 1938, pp. 141–51.

Canby, S.R., *Persian painting,* British Museum Press, London, 1993.
——*The rebellious reformer: the drawings and paintings of Riza-yi 'Abbasi of Isfahan,* Azimuth Editions, London, 1996.
——*The golden age of Persian art 1501 – 1722,* British Museum Press, London, 1999.
Carboni, S. and T. Masuya, *Persian Tiles ,* The Metropolitan Museum of Art, New York 1993
Contadini, A. & C. Burnett, *Islam and the Italian Renaissance, Warburg Institute Colloquia 5,* Warburg Institute, London, 1999.
Collon, Dominique (ed.), 7000 Years of Seals, British Museum Press, London, 1997.

Content, D., *Islamic rings and gems: the Benjamin Zucker Collection,* Philip Wilson Publishers, London, 1987.
Curtis, V. S., *Persian Myths,* British Museum Press, London 1993
Cragg, Kenneth (transl.), *Readings in the Quran,* Fount, London, 1988.

Cribb, J. Cook, B. and I. Carradice, *The Coin Atlas,* London 1990.
Cribb, J., *Magic coins of Java, Bali, and the Malay Peninsula: thirteenth to twentieth centuries: a catalogue based on the Raffles Collection of coin-shaped charms from Java in the British Museum,* British Museum Press, London, 1999.
Crill, Rosemary, *Arts of India* 1550-1900, Victoria and Albert Museum, London, 1990.

Critchlow, Keith, *Islamic Patterns,* Thames & Hudson, London, 2001.

D'Avennes, Prisse (ed.), *Arabia Art on Colour,* Dover Publications inc., New York, 1978.

Derman, U., *Letters of gold: Ottoman calligraphy from the Sakib Sabanci Collection, Istanbul,* the Metropolitan Museum of Art, New York, 1998.

Deroche, F., *The Abbasid tradition: Qur'ans of the 8th to 10th centuries,* Nour Foundation in assoc. with Azimuth Editions & Oxford University Press, London, 1992.
Dihlavi, H.Q., *Tadhkirat-i khvu shnivisan* (ed. Hidayat, M.H.) Asiatic Society, Calcutta, 1910
Dodge, B. (ed. & trans.), *The fihrist of Ibn al-Nadim,* 2 vols, Columbia University Press, New York, 1970.
Elgood, Robert, *Arms and Armour of Arabia in the 18th, 19th and 20th century,* Scolar Press, England, 1994.

Esposito, John L., *The Oxford History of Islam,* Oxford University Press, New York, 1999.

Ettinghausen, R., O. Grabar & M. Jenkins-Madina, *Islamic art and architecture 650 – 1250,* Yale University Press, New Haven & London, 2001.
Ettinghausen, R., 'Muslim decorative arts and painting, their nature and impact on the medieval West', in Ferber, S (ed.), *Islam and the medieval West,* New York, 1975.
Ferber, S., 'Islam and the medieval West', *Catalogue and papers of the ninth annual conference of the Center for Medieval and Early Renaissance Studies,* vol. 1, State University of New York, Binghamton, 1975.
Ferrier, R.W. (edt.), *Arts of Persia,* Yale University Press, New Heaven, 1989.

Frothingham, A.W., *Lustreware of Spain,* the Hispanic Society of America, New York, 1951.
Gaur, A., *A history of calligraphy,* Cross River Press, London, 1994.
Ghouchani, A, *Inscriptions on Nishapur pottery,* Reza Abbasi Museum, Tehran, 1986.
Godman, F.D., *The Godman Collection of Oriental and Spanish pottery and glass 1865 – 1900,* Taylor & Francis, London, 1901.
Gonzalez, Valerie, *Beauty and Islam – aesthetics in Islamic art and architecture,* I.B Tauris Publishers, London, 2001.

Grohmann, A., *Arabische paläographie,* 2 vols, Hermann Böhlaus Nachf, der Österreichischen Akademie der Wissenschaften, Vienna, 1971.
Grube, Ernest J., *Architecture of the Islamic World: its history and social meaning,* Thames and Hudson, 1995.

Guesdon, M.G. & A. Vernay-Nouri (eds), *L'art du livre Arabe,* Bibliothèque Nationale de France, Paris, 2001.
Harris, Jennifer (ed.), *5000 Years of Textiles,* British Museum Press, London, 1993.
Harrison-Hall, J., *Catalogue of late Yuan and Ming ceramics in the British Museum,* British

Museum Press, London, 2001.

El-Hawary, H. and H. Rached, *Les Steles funerarires,* vols 1 and 3, Cairo 1932-8

Healey, J., *The early alphabet,* British Museum Press, London, 1990.

Henzell-Thomas, J., *Where the two oceans meet: the art of Ahmed Moustafa,* Fe-Noon Ahmed Moustafa UK Ltd, London, 1998.

Hithcock, Michael, Indonesian Textiles, Periplus editions, Indonesia, 1991.

Hoare, O., The Calligraphers' Craft, London 1987

Hourani, A, *A history of the Arab peoples,* Faber and Faber, London, 1991.

Hoyland, R., *Arabia and the Arabs: from the Bronze Age to the coming of Islam,* Routledge, New York, 2001.

Ilyas, Mohammad, *Astronomy of Islamic Calendar,* A.S Noordeen, Kuala Lumpur, 1997.

Irving, Washington, *The Alhambra,* Darf Publishers Limited, London, 1986.

Irwin, R., *Islamic art,* Laurence King, London, 1997.

Ja'far, M., *Arabic calligraphy: naskh style for beginners,* British Museum Press, London, 2002.

James, D., *Qur'ans of the Mamluks,* Thames & Hudson, New York, 1988.

___ ___ , *After Timur,* Nour Foundation, 1991.

Johnstone, Penelope (transl.), *Medicine of the Prophet,* The Islamic Text Society, United Kingdom, 2001.

Kalus, L., *Catalogue des Cachets, Bulles et Talismans Islamiques ,* Bibliothèque Nationale, Paris 1981

Kerlogue, F., 'Islamic talismans: the calligraphy batiks', in A Van Hout (ed.), *Batik drawn in wax: 200 years of batik art from Indonesia in the Tropenmuseum Collection,* Royal Tropical Institute, Amsterdam, 2001.

Khalili, N.D, B.W. Robinson and T. Stanley, *Lacquer of the Islamic lands.* The Nasser David Khalili collection of Islamic Art vol. 22, Oxford University Press 1996

Khan, Dr. Muhammad Muhsin (transl.), *Sahih al-Bukhari,* Maktabah Darul Salam, Riyadh, 1994.

Khan, Gabriel Mandel, *Arabic Script,* Abbeville Press Publishers, New York, 2001.

Khan, Maulana Wahiduddin, *Religion and Science,* Goodword Books, New Delhi, 2000.

Khatibi, Abdelkebir, *The Splendour of Islamic Calligraphy,* Thames and Hudson, France, 1994.

'Khatt', *Encyclopaedia of Islam,* new edn, vol. IV, Brill, Leiden, 1978, pp. 1113–28.

'Kitabat', *Encyclopaedia of Islam,* new edn, vol. V, Brill, Leiden, 1986, pp. 210–33.

Komaroff, L. & S. Carboni, *The legacy of Genghis Khan, courtly art and culture in western Asia, 1256–1353*, the Metropolitan Museum of Art, New York, in assoc. with Yale University Press, New Haven & London, 2002.

Krahl, R., with N. Erbahar, *Chinese Ceramics in the Topkapi Saray Museum* (ed. J. Ayers) 3 vols. Sotheby's, London)1986

Kuhnel, Prof.Dr. Ernst, *Islamic Art of Calligraphy,* Heintze and Blanckertz, Berlin, 1942.

Kurkman, *G. Ottoman Silver Marks,* Istanbul, 1996.

Lane, A., *Later Islamic pottery,* Faber and Faber, London, 1957.

Lane-Poole, S., *Catalogue of Oriental coins in the British Museum,* vols I–X, The British Museum, London, 1875–90.

Laufer, B., 'Chinese Muhammedan bronzes with a study of the Arabic inscriptions by Martin Sprengling' *Ars Islamica* 1, 1934, 133-146

Lings, M. & Y. Safadi, *The Qur'an,* the World of Islam Publishing Company, London, 1976.

Long, Jean, *The Art of Chinese Calligraphy,* Dover PublicationsInc. New York, 2001.

Maddison, F. and E. Savage-Smith, *Science, Tools & Magic,* 2 vols. Nour Foundation in assoc. with Azimuth Editions & Oxford University Press, London, 1997.

Mahdar, Sayid Mustafar, *Al Madinah al Munawarah,* Thara'a Publications, Madinah, 1977.

Momtaz, Irene, *A Perspective of Unity,* Momtaz Islamic Art, London, 1997.

Mansour, N. ,

Massoudy, H, *Calligraphie Arabe vivante,* Flammarion, Paris, 1981.

Melikian-Chirvani, A.S., *Islamic metalwork from the Iranian world 8 – 18th centuries,* Victoria and Albert Museum, London, 1982.

___ ___, *Metal Work ,* Studia Islamica, 11, 1982.

___ ___, *"From the Royal Boat to the Begger's Bowl",* Islamic Art IV, 1991.

Minorsky, V., *Calligraphers and painters: a treatise by Qadi Ahmad, son of Mir Munshi (circa AH 1015/AD 1606). Freer Gallery of Art occasional paper,* Freer Gallery of Art, Washington DC, 1959.
Mitchiner, M., *The world of Islam: Oriental coins and their values,* Hawkins Publications, London, 1977.
Morton, A.H., *A catalogue of early Islamic glass stamps in the British Museum,* British Museum Press, London, 1985.
Nadir, A., *Imperial Ottoman Fermans,* London, 1986.
Nasr, Seyyed Hossein, *Islamic Art and Spirituality,* Golgonooza Press, Cambridge, 1987.
Plant, R., *Arabic coins and how to read them,* Seaby, London, 1973.
Pope, Arthur E., *A Survey of Persian Art,* Oxford University Press, New York, 1938.

Porter, V., *Islamic tiles,* British Museum Press, London, 1995.
——'Islamic seals: magical or practical?', in A Jones (ed.), *University lectures in Islamic studies, vol. 2, London, 1998.*
——forthcoming, *Arabic and Persian seals and amulets in the British Museum,* British Museum Press, London, 2005.
Rampuri, Syed, Ahmad, The History of Calligraphy, Rampur Raza Library, India, 1997.
Reinaud, M., *Monumens Arabes Persans et Turcs du cabinet de M le Duc de Blacas et d'autres cabinets,* 2 vols, Imprimerie Royale, Paris, 1828.
Robinson, Francis, Islamic World, Cambridge University Press, Melbourne, 1996.

Rogers, J.M., *Islamic art & design 1500 – 1700,* British Museum Publications, 1983.
——'The Godman Bequest of Islamic pottery', Apollo, July 1984, pp. 24–31.
Rogers, M. and R. Ward., *Sulayman the Magnificent,* British Museum Press, London 1988.
Sabr-ameli, Sayyid 'Abbas., *The Light of the Holy Quran,* Amirul –Mu'mineen Ali (a.s), Iran, 1998.

Safadi, Y.H., *Islamic calligraphy,* Thames & Hudson, London, 1978.
Safwat, NF, *The harmony of letters: Islamic calligraphy from the Tareq Rajab Museum,* National Heritage Board, Singapore, 1997.
Safwat, Nabil F., *Golden Pages,* Oxford University Press, New York, 2000.

Safwat, Nabil F., The Nasser D. Khalili Collection of Islamic Art – *The Art of the Pen,* The Nour Foundation, England, 1996.

Salameh, Khader, *The Quran Manuscript,* Garnet Publishing Limited, United Kingdom, 2001.

Schimmel, A, *Islamic calligraphy,* Brill, Leiden, 1970.
——*Calligraphy and Islamic culture,* New York University Press, 1990.
Schmitz, Barbara, *After the Great Moghuls,* Marg Publication, Mumbai, 2002.

Selheim, R, 'Die Madonna mit der Schahada', in E Graf (ed.), *Festschrift Werner* Caskel, Brill, Leiden, 1968.
Seven stories: about modern art in Africa, Whitechapel Art Gallery, London 1995
Shawa, L & A Wijdan, *Laila Shawa: the walls of Gaza, Wijdan calligraphic abstractions,* ex. cat., October Gallery, London, 1994.
Sinha, S, 'A note on the inscriptions of the Bengal Sultans in the British Museum', in E Haque (ed.), *Hakim Rahman Khan commemoration* volume, Dhaka, 2001.
Spink, M., (ed.) *Islamic jewellery,* Spink & Son, London, 1986.
Spring, C, *African arms and armour,* British Museum Press, London, 1993.
Stocchi, S. *Islam in prints,* Be-Ma Editrice, Milan 1988
Tabbaa,Y., 'The transformation of Arabic writing: part I, Qur'anic calligraphy', *Ars Orientalis,* vol. 21, 1991, pp. 119–48.
——'The transformation of Arabic writing: part 2, the public text', Ars Orientalis, vol. 24, 1994, pp. 119–47.
Terres secrètes de Samarqande, Institut du Monde Arabe, Paris 1992
Thornton, L., *Women as Portrayed in Orientalist Painting*, Paris, 1994.

Tournier, Michel, *Hassan Massoudy Calligraphe,* Flammarion, France, 1986.

Vajifdar, M., 'Materials and techniques of Islamic illuminations and bindings', in D.L. James (ed.), *Islamic masterpieces of the Chester Beatty Library,* World of Islam Festival Trust, London, 1981.
Walker, J., *A catalogue of the Arab-Sassanian coins,* British Museum Press, London,
Ward, R., *Islamic metalwork*, British Museum Press, London, 1993.

——& SC La Niece, DR Hook & R White, 'Veneto-Saracenic metalwork: an analysis of the bowls and incense burners in the British Museum', *Trade and discovery: the scientific study of artefacts from post-medieval Europe and beyond. British Museum occasional paper no. 109*, British Museum Press, London, 1995.

Watson, O., *Persian Lustre Ware* , Faber and Faber , London 1985

Whelan, E., '*Writing the word of God*: some early Qur'an manuscripts and their milieu, part I', Ars Orientalis, vol. 20, 1990, pp. 113–47.

1941.

Welch, Anthony, *Calligraphy in the Arts of the Muslim World,* Dawson, England, 1979.

Wiet, G. *Les stèles funéraires* vols. II and IV-X Musée Arabe, Cairo 1936-42

Wijdan, A., *Modern Islamic art: development and continuity*, University Press Florida, Gainesville, 1997.

Wilkinson, C.K., *Nishapur: Pottery of the Early Islamic Period*, The Metropolitan Museum of Art, Greenwhich Conn. 1973

Wright, W., '*Kufic tombstones in the British Museum*", Proceedings of the Society of biblical Archaeology, June 1887, 329-349.

_____, *Asian Costumes and Textiles* from Bosphorus to Fujiyama, Skira Editore, Italy, 2001.

_____, *Beijing Muslim, China Ethnic*, Photography, Art Publisher, Beijing, 1999.

_____, *Culture Treasures-Textiles of the Malay World,* National Museum of New Delhi, New Delhi, 2003.

_____, *Islamic Arts Museum of Malaysia,* Islamic Arts of Malaysia, Kuala Lumpur, 2000.

_____, *The Crafts of Malaysia,* Editions Didier Millet, Singapore, 1997.

_____, *The Unity of Islamic Art*, King Faisal Center for Research and Islamic Studies, Riyadh, 1985.

Websites

www.islamic-world.net/economic/waqf/waqf_mainpage.html

www.geocities.com/massad002/appendix2

www.usc.edu/dept/msa/reference/searchhadith.html

www.historicalextrarchive.com/section.php

www.tughranet.f2s.com/tughras/tughras.htm

www.metmuseum.org/explore/TUGHRA/tughra.html

www.alislam.org/library/links/00000212.html

www.islamicity.com/ps/default.asp

www.lesarturcs.com/calligraphy/intro.html

www.stars.com/art

www.iiu.edu.my/waqf/waqf.htm

www.geocities.com/islamicresourcecenter/islamicart.html

www.ezsoftech.com/hajj/hajj_article1.asp

www.quraan.com/Tafsir/TafseerAyatulUIKursi.asp

www.almujtaba.com/1/ayatalkursi.html

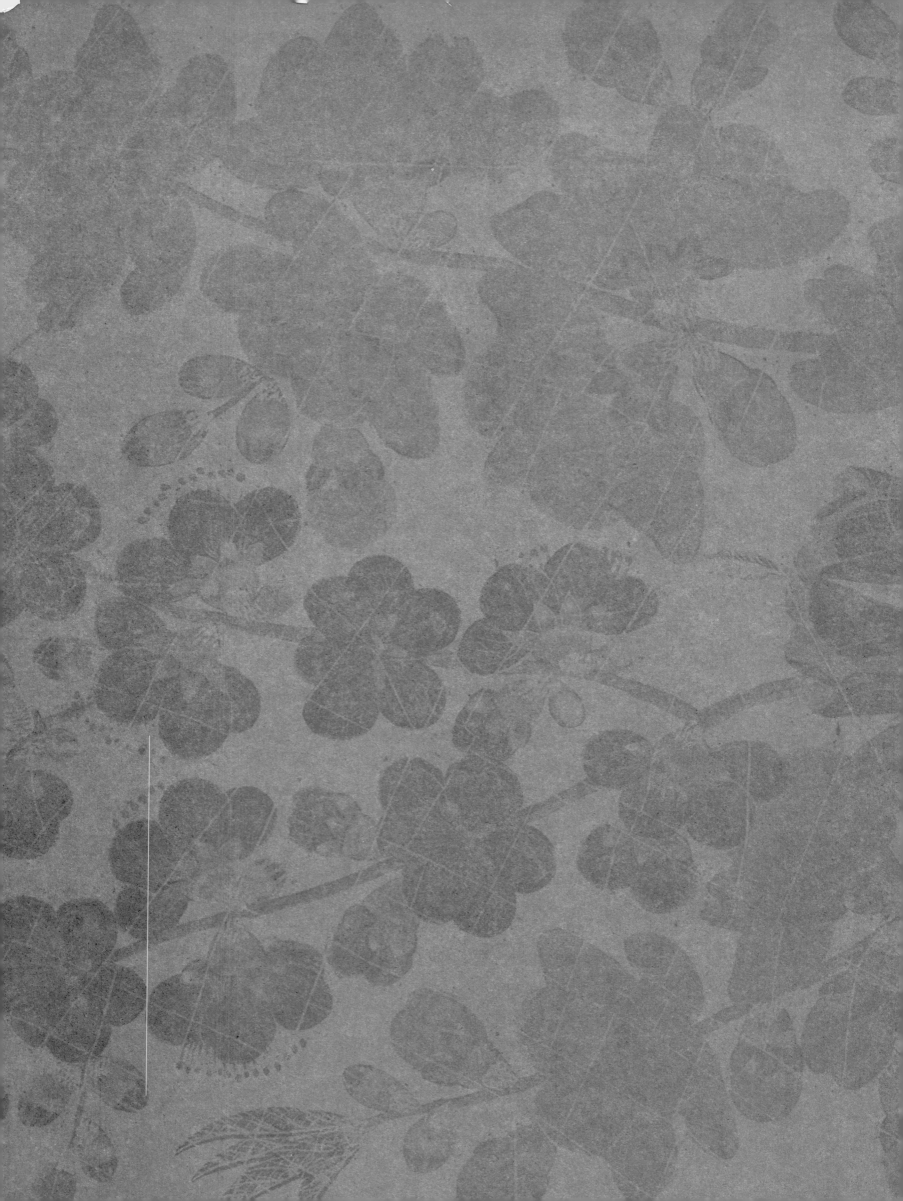